Technology Sourcebook

UCSMP
Secondary Component

THE UNIVERSITY OF CHICAGO SCHOOL MATHEMATICS PROJECT

PRECALCULUS AND DISCRETE MATHEMATICS

INTEGRATED MATHEMATICS

Using Technology

Computer Masters

Calculator Masters

Answers

Scott Foresman
Addison Wesley

Editorial Offices: Glenview, Illinois • Menlo Park, California
Sales Offices: Reading, Massachusetts • Atlanta, Georgia
Glenview, Illinois • Carrollton, Texas • Menlo Park, California

ISBN: 0-673-45922-5

http://www.sf.aw.com

1 2 3 4 5 6—ML—01 00 99 98

Contents

Using Technology in Your Classroom

Based upon the NCTM *Standards,* the University of Chicago School Mathematics Project is committed to using the power of technology to involve students in conceptually-oriented learning activities. The *Precalculus and Discrete Mathematics Technology Sourcebook* offers a wide variety of innovative student activities which use software tools and graphics calculators. In addition to the activities in this *Sourcebook*, there are activities integrated in the *Student Edition* and in *Explorations* software listed below. These activities are all referenced in the *Precalculus and Discrete Mathematics Teacher's Edition.*

Technology is changing so quickly. The functions of computers and calculators are becoming increasingly similar. Many Technology Masters presented as Computer Masters can be easily adapted for use with graphics calculators, or graphics calculators equipped with a table generator, statistics capability, or a symbolic manipulator. Use each master with the technology at hand, adapting as necessary.

SOURCEBOOK COMPONENTS
The three **Computer Masters** and nineteen **Calculator Masters** offer activities correlated to the *Precalculus and Discrete Mathematics* textbook. They provide activities for students to do independently or in small groups. The correlation chart on pages *v-vii* indicates the lessons for which there are activities in the Technology Sourcebook.

SOFTWARE FOR USE WITH COMPUTER MASTERS
You may want to use some of the following software tools, available from Scott Foresman-Addison Wesley. Commercial spreadsheet programs such as Microsoft® Excel may be used for spreadsheet activities. Computer drawing programs may be used for some masters.

GraphExplorer (Macintosh/IBM Compatibles)   A tool students can use to graph rectangular, conic, polar and parametric equations; zoom; transform functions; and experiment with families of equations.

f(g) Scholar (Macintosh/Windows)   A very powerful mathematics program that combines a spreadsheet, graphing tool, statistics features, a calculation window, and hundreds of built-in functions.

Other Software for Precalculus and Discrete Mathematics

Explorations CD-ROM (Macintosh/Windows)   Offers interactive examples and explorations for teacher demonstrations or student use. Explorations were designed to be used directly with 40 lessons and In-class Activities in *Precalculus and Discrete Mathematics.*

TestWorks CD-ROM (Macintosh/Windows)   Includes a database of questions for each objective, along with numerous prepared tests and quizzes for each chapter. Also includes challenge problems.

Correlation Chart

Text Lesson or Pages	Component	Drawing Program	GraphExplorer	Spreadsheet	Calculator	Recommended Use/Comments
Chapter 1: Mathematics and Logical Reasoning						
1–3	Computer Master 1, Logic and Spreadsheets			■		Lesson extension.
Chapter 2: Analyzing Functions						
2–2	Calculator Master 1, Turning Points of Graphs of Polynomial Functions		■		■	Lesson extension; this master could also be adapted for use with GraphExplorer.
2–4	Calculator Master 2, Exploring End Behavior		■		■	Lesson follow-up; this master could also be adapted for use with GraphExplorer.
2–5	Calculator Master 3, Parametrics and Projectiles		■		■	Lesson follow-up; this master could also be adapted for use with GraphExplorer.
Chapter 3: Functions, Equations, and Inequalities						
3–7	Calculator Master 4, Solving Inequalities Graphically		■		■	Lesson introduction or follow-up; this master could also be adapted for use with GraphExplorer
Chapter 4: Integers and Polynomials						
4–2	Calculator Master 5, The Remainder Theorem		■		■	Lesson follow-up; this master could also be adapted for use with GraphExplorer.
4–3	Calculator Master 6, Dividing Polynomials				■	Lesson follow-up.
4–7	Calculator Master 7, Factors and Prime Numbers				■	Lesson extension and follow-up.

Text Lesson or Pages	Component	Drawing Program	GraphExplorer	Spreadsheet	Calculator	Recommended Use/Comments
Chapter 5: Rational Numbers and Rational Functions						
5–5	Calculator Master 8, Simple Sequences with Complex Behavior		■		■	Lesson extension; this master could also be adapted for use with GraphExplorer.
5–8	Calculator Master 9, Solving Rational Equations Graphically		■		■	Lesson follow-up; this master could also be adapted for use with GraphExplorer.
5–9	Computer Master 2, Drawing Escher-Style Tessellations	■				Lesson follow-up.
Chapter 6: Trigonometric Identities and Equations						
6–3	Computer Master 3, Parametric Equations and Ellipses		■		■	Lesson extension; this master could also be adapted for use with a calculator with graphing capabilities.
6–5	Calculator Master 10, Testing and Proving Identities		■		■	Lesson follow-up; this master could also be adapted for use with GraphExplorer.
Chapter 7: Recursion and Mathematical Induction						
7–1	Calculator Master 11, Simple Sequences with Complex Behavior				■	Lesson extension.
Chapter 8: Polar Coordinates and Complex Numbers						
8–5	Calculator Master 12, Families of Polar Graphs		■		■	Lesson follow-up; this master could also be adapted for use with GraphExplorer.
Chapter 9: The Derivative in Calculus						
9–2	Calculator Master 13, Secant Lines and Tangent Lines				■	Lesson follow-up.
Chapter 10: Combinatorics						
10–2	Calculator Master 14, Lotteries				■	Lesson extension.
10–6	Calculator Master 15, Simulating Binomial Experiments				■	Lesson extension.

Precalculus and Discrete Mathematics © Scott Foresman Addison Wesley

Name _____

COMPUTER MASTER 1

Software: *Spreadsheet*

The rules of *and* and *or* studied in your text have many practical applications in spreadsheets, networks, and other computer programming. In this activity you will see that AND and OR functions can be used to indicate which operations a spreadsheet executes.

1. **Defining the Problem** Suppose Mid-Rivers College offers both regular and honors programs to incoming freshmen depending on their ACT or total SAT scores. The criteria for the honors program is as follows:

   At least 28 ACT composite *or* at least 1300 total SAT

   a. Set up a spreadsheet with the following student data.

	A	B	C	D	E	F
1	Student	ACT comp.	SAT verbal	SAT math	%ile rank	Hon. or Reg.
2	Russo, J.	24	620	781	88	
3	O'Hare, P.	29	520	590	94	
4	Herrera, H.	27	600	615	91	
5	Krutz, W.	30			97	
6	Chin, E.		788	683	90	
7	Lyon, L.	31	675	662	89	

   b. With hundreds of records such as these, it may be desirable to have a computer quickly determine the appropriate program, honors or regular, for each student.

   In cell F2, enter the formula below and fill down through cell F7.

   =IF(OR(B2>=28,C2+D2>=1300),"honors","regular")

   The two *arguments* of the OR function are given in parentheses separated by a comma. Hence, OR(B2>=28,C2+D2>=1300) means $B2 \geq 28$ *or* $C2+D2 \geq 1300$.

   c. Which of the seven students qualify for the honors program? _____

   d. In terms of B2, C2, and D2, when is the OR function true in this IF statement?

   _____

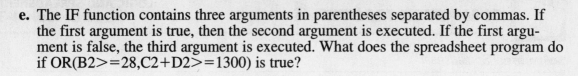

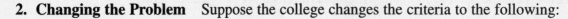

e. The IF function contains three arguments in parentheses separated by commas. If the first argument is true, then the second argument is executed. If the first argument is false, the third argument is executed. What does the spreadsheet program do if OR(B2>=28,C2+D2>=1300) is true?

_____

2. Changing the Problem Suppose the college changes the criteria to the following:

At least 28 ACT composite *and* at least 1300 total SAT

a. In cell F2, enter the formula below and fill down through F7.

=IF(AND(B2>=28,C2+D2>=1300),"honors","regular")

In this formula, AND(B2>=28,C2+D2>=1300) means B2≥28 *and* C2+D2≥1300.

b. Now which of the seven students qualify for the honors program? _____

c. In terms of B2, C2, and D2, when is the AND function true in this IF statement?

_____

d. What does the spreadsheet program do if AND(B2>=28,C2+D2>=1300) is false?

_____

3. Considering a Similar Problem Suppose Mt. Whiting University uses the following criteria to place students in the honors program:

At least 90%ile class rank *and* either at least 27 ACT composite *or* at least 1250 total SAT

a. In cell F2, enter a formula to determine whether a student is offered the honors or regular program. Fill down through cell F7. What formula did you enter?

_____

b. Which of the seven students qualify for Mt. Whiting's honors program? _____

Precalculus and Discrete Mathematics © Scott Foresman Addison Wesley

COMPUTER MASTER 2

Software: *Graphic art*

In Lesson 5-9 you read about the various regular polygons that tessellate the plane. Other polygons, such as rectangles and parallelograms, also tessellate the plane. The graphic artist M. C. Escher (1898–1972) drew many fascinating tessellations of the plane based on a variety of these polygons. He incorporated reflections, rotations, translations, and glide-reflections, which you probably studied in earlier courses. Modern-day art software makes it possible to draw this type of pattern with great precision.

The first pattern developed below is based on an equilateral triangle and incorporates glide reflections. If your software allows you to work in layers, the specific layers will be indicated in parentheses. Use the zoom tool to ensure a precise drawing. Do not label your picture. The labels shown below are provided only to clarify these instructions.

Step 1 (Layer 1) Draw an equilateral triangle about 2 to 3 inches on a side. Zoom in so it fills at least a quarter of the screen.

Step 2 (Layer 2) Show guides or a grid to locate the midpoint *M* of *AB*. Use a pencil or curve tool to draw a curve from *A* to *M*.

Step 3 (Layer 2) Copy the curve and paste it anywhere in the drawing. Then select the copy, flip it horizontally, and move it so it fits from *M* to *B*.

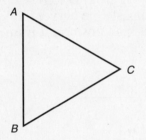

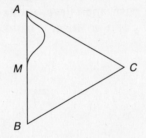

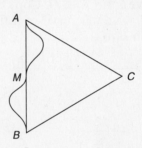

Step 4 (Layer 3) Draw a curve from *A* to *C*.

Step 5 (Layer 3) Copy and paste the curve. Then select it, flip it horizontally, and move it so it fits precisely from *C* to *B*.

Step 6 (Layer 4) Draw in some details. Delete the triangle (or hide or delete Layer 1). Then copy the completed figure onto a new canvas (or merge Layers 2, 3, and 4).

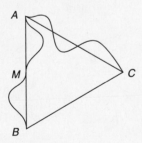

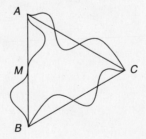

Step 7 (New layer)   To draw the tessellation, copy the figure, paste it anywhere, select it, and flip it horizontally. Then move it so it fits precisely with the original figure. Continue copying and pasting the figure to fill the canvas, flipping alternate copies. Color or shade as desired.

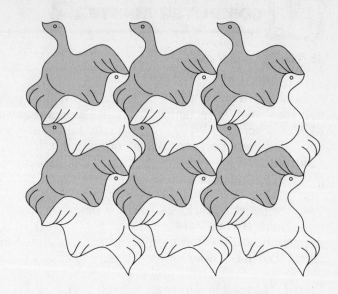

The next pattern is based on a rectangle and incorporates translations and rotations.

Step 1 (Layer 1)   Draw a rectangle about 3 inches long. (Layer 2) Draw a curve from *A* to *D*. Copy and paste the curve so it fits from *B* to *C*.

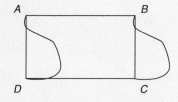

Step 2 (Layer 3)   Locate the midpoint *M* of $\overline{AB}$. Draw a curve from *A* to *M*. Copy and paste the curve, rotate it 180°, and position it from *B* to *M*.

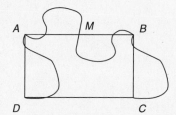

Step 3 (Layer 4)   Locate the midpoint *N* of $\overline{CD}$. Draw a curve from *D* to *N*. Copy and paste the curve, rotate it 180° and position it from *C* to *N*.

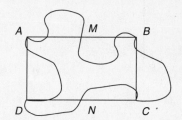

Step 7 (Layer 5)   Draw in some details and delete the rectangle (or its layer).

(New Layer) Draw the tessellation by copying and pasting the figure, rotating some copies 180°.

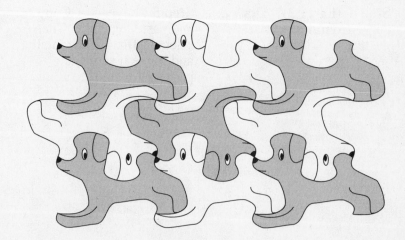

1. Design your own tessellation based on a different polygon.

2. Design your own tessellation based on either using rotations and an equilateral triangle or glide-reflections and a rectangle.

Precalculus and Discrete Mathematics © Scott Foresman Addison Wesley

COMPUTER MASTER 3

Software: *GraphExplorer or similar software; graphics calculator*

In Lesson 6-3, you saw that the graph of the parametric equations $\begin{cases} x = \cos t \\ y = \sin t \end{cases}$ is a circle centered at (0, 0) with radius 1. In this investigation you will examine the effects of applying various transformations to this pair of parametric equations.

1. **Setting the Window** Set your graphing utility to parametric and radian modes. Graph the parametric equations given above for $0 \le t \le 2\pi$, in the window $-8 \le x \le 8$, $-5 \le y \le 5$. GraphExplorer does not ask for the t-step. On a calculator use a t-step of .1. On a calculator, your circle might appear elongated. If so, use the zoom square feature to adjust the window so the graph appears as a true circle.

2. **Using the Pythagorean Identity to Verify Graphs** Now graph $\begin{cases} x = 2\cos t \\ y = 2\sin t \end{cases}$.

   a. Describe the graph. _____

   b. Prove your answer to part **a** by squaring both sides of the equations, adding them, and then simplifying by using the Pythagorean identity.

   _____

   _____

   c. Predict the graph of $\begin{cases} x = 3\cos t \\ y = 3\sin t \end{cases}$. _____

   Then graph the equations to check your prediction.

   d. Describe the graph of $\begin{cases} x = a\cos t \\ y = a\sin t \end{cases} a \ne 0.$ _____

3. **Applying Rubberband Transformations** Graph $\begin{cases} x = 2\cos t \\ y = 3\sin t \end{cases}$.

   a. Describe the graph. _____

   b. Prove your answer to part **a**. (Hint: Solve the first equation for cos *t* and the second equation for sin *t*. Then proceed as in Question **2b**.) _____

   _____

   _____

c. Predict the graph

of $\begin{cases} x = 4 \cos t - 1 \\ y = 3 \sin t + 2 \end{cases}$. _____

d. Check your prediction. Then prove that these parametric equations yield the figure shown in your graph.

_____

_____

e. Describe the graph of $\begin{cases} x = a \cos t + h \\ y = b \sin t + k \end{cases}$ $a \neq 0, b \neq 0$.

_____

4. Rotating the Graph Now graph $\begin{cases} x = \cos\left(t + \frac{\pi}{4}\right) \\ y = \sin t \end{cases}$.

a. Describe the graph. _____

b. You might recall from earlier courses that if the axes of an ellipse are not parallel to the x and y axes, its equation typically contains an xy term. Show that this pair of parametric equations is equivalent to the quadratic equation $x^2 + \sqrt{2}xy + y^2 - \frac{1}{2} = 0$. (Hint: Begin with the identity for $\cos(\alpha + \beta)$.) If you are using *GraphExplorer*, you can click on Conic in the Advanced mode and graph this equation. The graph should be the same as that of part **a**.

_____

_____

c. Predict the graph of $\begin{cases} x = \cos\left(t - \frac{\pi}{2}\right) \\ y = \sin t \end{cases}$. _____

d. Check your prediction. Explain why these parametric equations yield the figure shown.

_____

_____

Precalculus and Discrete Mathematics © Scott Foresman Addison Wesley

CALCULATOR MASTER 1

Calculator: *Graphics; GraphExplorer or similar software*

A **turning point** in the graph of a function is a point where the function changes from

increasing to decreasing or from decreasing to increasing ⌣ .

The number of possible turning points in the graph of a real polynomial function is related to the degree of the polynomial. For a polynomial of a given degree, how many turning points are possible?

1. **Exploring Graphs** In the middle column of the table below, write several more functions of the specified degree. Then graph each set of polynomial functions, one at a time, on your graphing calculator. Record the numbers of turning points you observe. Adjust your window as you search for all possible turning points and zoom in if it is not clear whether or not a point is a turning point.

Degree	Functions to Graph	Numbers of Turning Points Observed
1st	$y = 3x + 1$	
2nd	$y = x^2$ $y = -\frac{2}{3}x^2 + 5$ $y = 2x^2 + 3x - 8$	
3rd	$y = x^3$ $y = (x - 3)^3$	
4th	$y = -x^4 + 8$ $y = -x^4 + 2x^3 - x^2 + 3x + 1$	
5th	$y = x^5 - 3x^3$ $y = 2x^5 - 9x^4 + 6x^3 + 10x^2 - 2x - 4$	

2. **Analyzing Observations** Consider the graphs of the functions in Item **1**.

   a. Can a quadratic ever have zero turning points? _____

   b. Can a cubic ever have exactly one turning point? _____

   c. Explain how the number of turning points relates to the number of relative maxima and minima of a polynomial function.

   _____

   _____

3. **Making Predictions** Predict all the possible number of turning points for the graph of a polynomial function of the given degree.

   a. 6th degree _____

   b. 7th degree _____

   c. 8th degree _____

   d. 9th degree _____

   e. 10th degree _____

   f. Could a 100th-degree polynomial function have exactly six turning points? Explain.

   _____

   g. Could a 101st-degree polynomial function have exactly two turning points? Explain.

   _____

   h. Based on your observations, what is the maximum number of turning points for a polynomial function of nth degree? What is the minimum number of turning points? Consider whether n is even or odd in your answer.

   _____

4. **Writing Equations** Write an equation for a 6th-degree polynomial function with

   a. three turning points. _____

   b. five turning points. _____

Name _____

CALCULATOR MASTER 2

Calculator: *Graphics with table capability; GraphExplorer or similar software*

Graphs and tables can be used to determine the end behavior of a function. You need to be aware of the possible limitations of these aids.

1. **Examining End Behavior** Consider the function
$f(x) = 0.1x^5 + 1.2x^4 - x^3 - 12x^2 + x + 11.$

   a. Graph f in a window with $-5 \leq x \leq 5$ and $-5 \leq y \leq 5$.
   Can you observe the end behavior? _____

   b. Change the window so that $-10 \leq x \leq 10$ and $-20 \leq y \leq 20$. Describe the end behavior of f that is displayed.

   _____

   c. Change the window so that $-20 \leq x \leq 20$ and $-3000 \leq y \leq 3000$. Describe the end behavior of f that is displayed.

   _____

   d. Are your answers to parts **b** and **c** the same? Explain why or why not.

   _____

   e. Examine a table of values of $y = f(x)$ on your calculator. Let x get "very big" and then "very small" as shown in the chart below. Record the corresponding y-values. Do the values you record below support your conclusions in part **c**? Explain.

   _____

x	*y*
1000	
1001	
10000	
10001	
100000	
100001	

x	*y*
-1000	
-999	
-10000	
-9999	
-100000	
-99999	

2. **Studying Another Function** Consider the function
   $g(x) = 0.1x^4 + 0.63x^3 - 42.38x^2 + 88.95x - 20$.

   a. Graph g in a window with $-10 \le x \le 10$ and $-50 \le y \le 50$. Describe the end behavior of g that is displayed.

   _____

   b. Change the window so that $-20 \le x \le 20$ and $-50 \le y \le 50$. Describe the end behavior of g that is displayed.

   _____

   c. Change the window so that $-20 \le x \le 20$ and $-10000 \le y \le 10000$. Describe the end behavior of g that is displayed.

   _____

   d. Explain any differences in your answers to parts **a**, **b**, and **c**.

   _____

   e. Examine a table of values on your calculator to complete the chart below. Do the values you record support your conclusions in part **c**? Explain why or why not.

   _____

x	y
1000	
1001	
10000	
10001	
100000	
100001	

x	y
-1000	
-999	
-10000	
-9999	
-100000	
-99999	

3. **Evaluating the Methods** Which seems more reliable in helping to determine the end behavior of a function, graphs or tables? Explain your answer.

   _____

Precalculus and Discrete Mathematics © Scott Foresman Addison Wesley

Name _____

CALCULATOR MASTER 3

Calculator: *Graphics calculator with parametric mode; GraphExplorer*

The *x*- and *y*-coordinates of a golf ball launched from its tee, with a wind blowing in from the fairway, can be given as functions of a single variable *t*, where *t* is time (in seconds).

Let $x = d(t)$ represent the horizontal distance and $y = h(t)$ represent the height at time *t*. Then

$$d(t) = (v_o \cos \theta)t - v_w t \qquad \text{and} \qquad h(t) = -16t^2 + (v_o \sin \theta)t$$

where v_o = the initial velocity of the ball in ft/sec, v_w = the wind speed in ft/sec, and θ = the angle (from the horizontal) at which the golf ball is launched.

Consider the following situation.

A 6-mph wind is coming in from the fairway as Lyon Forrest tees up 150 yards away from hole #18. Lyon hits the ball at an angle of 10° with an initial velocity of 200 feet per second.

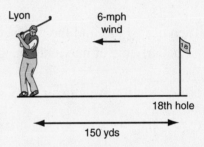

1. **Determining Equations** Lyon's situation can be modeled with equations.

   a. First identify v_o, θ, and v_w. Be careful. You need to change units to determine v_w.

   $v_o =$ _____ $\theta =$ _____ $v_w =$ _____

   b. Write parametric equations for Lyon's golf ball based on the information in part **a.**

   $d(t) =$ _____ $h(t) =$ _____

2. **Graphing and Analyzing the Path** Enter your equations into your calculator in parametric and degree modes. Graph using the following window.

Tmin = 0	Xmin = 0	Ymin = 0
Tmax = 3	Xmax = 500	Ymax = 50
Tstep = 0.1	Xscl = 50	Yscl = 5

   Use the trace key to track the flight of the ball.

a. How far does the ball land from the hole? Be careful: You need to consider the distance in *feet* of the tee from the hole. Tell about how far the ball travels in the air.

_____

b. To the nearest tenth, after how many seconds
does the ball hit the ground?   _____

c. What is the approximate maximum height of the ball?   _____

d. After how many seconds does the ball reach
the maximum height?   _____

e. To verify your answers to parts **a** through **d**,
compute the total time (in seconds) of flight
with the following formula:

$$t_{total} = \frac{v_o \sin \theta}{16} = \text{_____}$$

Then use t_{total} to find the distance the ball travels
in the air, time of maximum height, and the maximum height.

distance ball travels in air $= (v_o \cos \theta)t_{total} - v_w t_{total} =$ _____

$t_{max} = \frac{1}{2}t_{total} =$ _____   max height $= -16(t_{max})^2 + (v_o \sin \theta)t_{max} =$ _____

f. What if the wind dies? Adjust your equation
for $d(t)$ by deleting $v_w t$ and regraph. How
far does the ball land from the hole?   _____

g. Use the formulas in part **e** to find the distance the ball travels in the air and
maximum height of the ball with no wind.

distance ball travels in air $=$ _____   max height $=$ _____

3. **Making Predictions** How can Lyon adjust his swing to sink the ball?

a. Suppose Lyon still aims directly at the hole and hits the ball at a 10° angle.
Experiment with your equations to find the initial velocity that would cause
the ball to fall directly into the hole (no bounces or rolls) under the following
wind conditions.

6-mph hour wind: $v_o =$ _____   no wind: $v_o =$ _____

Use your graph to test your choices for the initial velocity, then verify your answers

Precalculus and Discrete Mathematics © Scott Foresman Addison Wesley

by using the formulas to find the distance the ball travels in the air.

b. Compare both sets of equations, with wind and without wind, from part **a**. Which ball has a higher maximum height, the one that fights the wind or the one that doesn't? What is the difference between the maximum heights of the two balls?

_____

c. Suppose Lyon still aims directly at the hole and hits the ball with an initial velocity of 200 ft/sec. Experiment to find the angle needed under the following wind conditions to make the ball fall directly into the hole.

6-mph hour wind: $\theta =$ _____   no wind: $\theta =$ _____

Use your graph to test your choices for the angle. Then verify your answers by using the formulas to find the distance the ball travels in the air.

d. Compare both sets of equations, with wind and without wind, from part **c**. Which ball has a higher maximum height, the one that fights the wind or the one that doesn't? What is the difference between the maximum heights of the two paths?

_____

4. **Using a Formula for Still Air** If there is no wind, the distance *r* the ball travels in the air is given by $r = \dfrac{v_o^2 \sin 2\theta}{32}$.

a. For what value of θ is the distance the ball travels in the air the greatest?   _____

b. Find the maximum distance the ball travels in the air if Lyon hits it with an initial velocity of 200 ft/sec. _____

c. Find the initial velocity at which Lyon should hit the ball in order for it to fall directly into the hole if he hits with the angle from part **a**.   _____

d. Adjust your equations (with no wind) to include the initial velocity from part **c** and the angle from part **a**. What is the time of flight for this ball?   _____

e. Adjust your Tmax and then graph the equations in part **d**. What do you notice about this path of the ball? _____

f. What is the maximum height of the ball in part **h**? _____

_____

CALCULATOR MASTER 4

Calculator: *Graphics; GraphExplorer or similar software*

Graphs can be used to solve inequalities in one variable by graphing a function in two variables. This technique can be valuable when other methods fail.

1. **Solving an Inequality** Consider the inequality
   $1.2x^4 - 1.34x^3 - 14.17x^2 + 13.36x + 4.2 > 0$.

   a. Write a corresponding function
   to be graphed. $f(x) =$ _____

   b. Graph the function in a standard
   window and determine the zeros of
   the function.   zeros: _____

   c. Determine for what intervals the function is positive and what intervals the function
   is negative.

   $f(x) > 0$ on the intervals _____

   $f(x) < 0$ on the intervals _____

   d. Use part **c** to solve the inequality and
   graph the solutions on a number line.   solutions: _____

   graph: ⟵————————————————————————⟶

2. **Solving Another Inequality** Consider the inequality $0.8x^3 + 0.2 \le 1.1x - x^2$.
   Repeat the procedure in Item **1**. (Hint: First set one side of the inequality to zero.)

   a. $g(x) =$ _____   **b.** zeros: _____

   c. $g(x) \ge 0$ on the intervals _____

   $g(x) \le 0$ on the intervals _____

   d. solutions: _____

   graph: ⟵————————————————————————⟶

Precalculus and Discrete Mathematics © Scott Foresman Addison Wesley

Repeat the procedure in Item **1** for each of the inequalities below.

3. $\dfrac{r^2 - 2.7r - 10.08}{r^2 + 2r + 3} \geq 0$

    a. $h(r) = $ _____

    b. zeros: _____

    c. $h(r) \geq 0$ on the intervals _____

        $h(r) \leq 0$ on the intervals _____

    d. solutions: _____

        graph: ⟵――――――――――――――――⟶

4. $5^{x^2} > 3^{(x+2)}$ (Hint: See hint for Item **2**.)

    a. $t(x) = $ _____

    b. zeros: _____

    c. $t(x) > 0$ on the intervals _____

        $t(x) < 0$ on the intervals _____

    d. solutions: _____

        graph: ⟵――――――――――――――――⟶

5. $(x + 1)\log_2 x < x^2 \log_5 x$ (Hint: See hint for Item **2**, and use the change of base formula to enter on your calculator $\log_2 x = \dfrac{\log(x)}{\log(2)}$.

    a. $u(x) = $ _____

    b. zeros: _____

    c. $u(x) > 0$ on the intervals _____

        $u(x) < 0$ on the intervals _____
        (Be careful. Examine the domain of u.)

    d. solutions: _____

        graph: ⟵――――――――――――――――⟶

Precalculus and Discrete Mathematics © Scott Foresman Addison Wesley

CALCULATOR MASTER 5

Calculator: *Graphics with table capability; GraphExplorer or similar software*

You can investigate the Remainder Theorem graphically. Consider each function f defined below as the quotient of two functions, that is, $f(x) = \dfrac{p(x)}{d(x)}$, where $d(x) = x - c$.

1. **Graphing the Function** Let $f(x) = \dfrac{2x^2 + x - 1}{x - 1}$.

   a. Graph f in a window with $-10 \le x \le 10$ and $-20 \le y \le 20$.

   b. State the domain of f. _____

   c. What is the value of c? _____

2. **Examining a Table** Examine a table of values on your calculator, starting at $x = 1$ and increasing x-values by 1.

   a. Does $f(x)$ seem linear over the domain
   you have picked? _____

   b. Change the table so it starts at $x = 1000$, increasing
   x-values by 1. Record the values in the chart below.
   Does $f(x)$ seem linear over the domain you have picked? _____

   c. Change the table so it starts at $x = -1000$, increasing
   x-values by 1. Record the values in the chart below.
   Does $f(x)$ seem linear over the domain you have picked? _____

x	y
1000	
1001	
1002	

x	y
-1000	
-999	
-998	

3. **Describing the Function at its Extremes** Examine the two tables above.

   a. What is the slope of the line containing the six points? _____

   b. Find an equation for the linear function q that
   contains the six points. $q(x) =$ _____

Precalculus and Discrete Mathematics © Scott Foresman Addison Wesley

c. Graph f and q in the window from Item **1**.
What do you notice? _____

4. **Relating to the Remainder Theorem** The Remainder Theorem, discussed in
Lesson 5–3, states $p(x) = q(x) \cdot (x - c) + p(c)$.

a. Given $f(x) = \dfrac{p(x)}{x - c}$ from Item **1** and $q(x)$ from **3b**, write out this statement for this
set of functions.

_____ = _____ · _____ + $p(\underline{\hspace{1cm}})$

b. Explain in your own words the significance of the linear equation you found in **3b**.

_____

c. Evaluate $p(c)$ for $c = 1$. _____

d. Using the value of $p(1)$ you found in part **c**, show that the two sides of the equation
in part **a** are equivalent.

_____

e. If $x \neq c$, then $p(x) = q(x) \cdot (x - c) + p(c)$ is equivalent to $\dfrac{p(x)}{x - c} = q(x) + \dfrac{p(c)}{x - c}$.
Write the instance of this statement for these functions.

_____ = _____ + _____

f. Graph $h(x) = q(x) + \dfrac{p(c)}{x - c}$.
Compare this graph with the graph of f. _____

g. Is $x - c$ a factor of $p(x)$? Explain your answer. _____

5. **Examining Another Function** Repeat **1a**, **1b**, and **1c** for the function
$f(x) = \dfrac{2x^2 + x - 1}{x + 1}$.

b. _____ **c.** _____

6. **Analyzing the Function** Repeat **2a**, **2b**, and **2c** for the function in Item **5**. The tables
are on the next page.

a. _____ **b.** _____ **c.** _____

x	y
1000	
1001	
1002	

x	y
-1000	
-999	
-998	

d. Find an equation for the linear function q that contains the six points you recorded above.　　$q(x) =$ _____

e. Given $f(x) = \dfrac{p(x)}{x - c}$ from Item **5** and $q(x)$ from part **d**, write out The Remainder Theorem for this set of functions.

_____ $=$ _____ $\cdot$ _____ $+ p($____$)$

f. Evaluate $p(-1)$ and show that the two sides of the equation in part **e** are equivalent.

_____

g. Write the instance of $\dfrac{p(x)}{x - c} = q(x) + \dfrac{p(c)}{x - c}$ for these functions.

_____ $=$ _____ $+$ _____

h. Graph $h(x) = q(x) + \dfrac{p(c)}{x - c}$.
Compare this graph with the graph of f.　　_____

i. Is $x - c$ a factor of $p(x)$? Explain your answer.　　_____

j. How you can tell graphically if $x - c$ is a factor of a quadratic polynomial $p(x)$?

_____

7. Analyzing Other Functions Repeat the analysis to complete parts **a**, **b**, and **c** below.

a. $f(x) = \dfrac{-2x^2 - 5x - 6}{x + 2}$　　$q(x) =$ ____　$p(c) =$ ____　Is $x - c$ a factor? ____

b. $f(x) = \dfrac{3x^2 + 5x - 2}{x + 1}$　　$q(x) =$ ____　$p(c) =$ ____　Is $x - c$ a factor? ____

c. $f(x) = \dfrac{-3x^2 + 7x - 2}{x - 2}$　　$q(x) =$ ____　$p(c) =$ ____　Is $x - c$ a factor? ____

Precalculus and Discrete Mathematics © Scott Foresman Addison Wesley

Calculator: *Programmable*

Synthetic division can be used to divide a polynomial $p(x)$ by a first-degree binomial $d(x)$ with a leading coefficient of 1. The following program performs such division of polynomials and displays the coefficients of the quotient $q(x)$ and the remainder $r(x)$ as a list. (The program is shown in two columns to save space.)

```
PROGRAM: SYNTHDIV
  : ClrHome                            : C→L1(P)
  : Input "DIVISOR CONSTANT:",K        : End
  : Input "DIVIDEND DEGREE:",E         : ClrHome
  : E+1→E                              : L1(1)→L3(1)
  : E→dim(L1)                          : For(P,1,E−1,1)
  : E→dim(L2)                          : L3(P)*K→L2(P+1)
  : E→dim(L3)                          : L1(P+1)−L2(P+1)→L3(P+1)
  : FOR (P,1,E,1)                      : End
  : Input "COEF:",C                    : Disp L3
```

1. **Using the Program** Enter the program SYNTHDIV. When you run the program, you will be asked to enter the constant of $d(x)$. Then you will be asked to enter the degree of $p(x)$ and its coefficients in standard order, one at a time.

   The coefficients of the quotient $q(x)$ will be displayed in standard order in a list. The last element of the list will be the remainder, a constant. For example, the list {2 -3 0 4 -5} represents a quotient of $2x^3 - 3x^2 + 4$ and a remainder of -5.

   Run the program to divide $2x^3 - 13x + 12$ by $x + 3$. Be sure to enter the coefficients of the dividend in order and enter 0 for the coefficient of each missing term.

   a. What are the coefficients of the quotient? _____

   b. Give $q(x)$. _____

   c. Give $r(x)$. _____

2. **Doing Other Divisions** Run the program to determine $q(x)$ and $r(x)$ when $p(x)$ is divided by $d(x)$. If you cannot see all of the entries in L3, access L3 and then scroll.

   a. $p(x) = 4x^5 - 9x^4 + 3x^3 - 5x^2 + 8x - 5;\ d(x) = x - 2$

   _____

b. $p(x) = 4x^4 - x^2 - 2x + 1; d(x) = x - \dfrac{1}{2}$

_____

c. In either part **a** or part **b**, is $d(x)$ a factor of $p(x)$? How can you tell?

_____

3. **Adjusting for Other Divisors** Consider $\dfrac{p(x)}{d(x)} = \dfrac{3x^4 + x^3 - 18x^2 - 3x + 8}{3x + 1}$.

    a. Explain why the program SYNTHDIV cannot perform this division directly.

_____

    b. If both the numerator and denominator are divided by 3, the result is an equivalent division. Why does this allow you to use SYNTHDIV?

_____

    c. Divide the numerator and denominator by 3. Then use the resulting coefficients to run SYNTHDIV. Give $q(x)$.

_____

    d. The remainder shown must be multiplied by 3 to give the correct remainder, $r(x)$, for the original division. Give $r(x)$.   _____

4. **Editing the Program** You can follow the technique in Item **3** to edit SYNTHDIV to allow for divisors with any nonzero leading coefficient.

    a. Edit the program with the following changes:

        (1) After the second line, insert an Input statement that asks for the coefficient of x in the divisor. (Call it A.)

        (2) Replace C with C/A in the statement C→L1(P).

        (3) Replace K with K/A in the statement L3(P)*K→L2(P+1).

        (4) Just above the last statement insert the statement K*L3(E)→L3(E).

    b. Test your new program on the original division given in Item **3**. If you do not get the same results for $q(x)$ and $r(x)$, try to fix your program.

    c. Divide $3x^5 - 38x^4 + 24x^3 + 6x - 20$ by $3x - 2$. Give $q(x)$ and $r(x)$.

_____

Name _____

Calculator: *Programmable*

From at least the time of Pythagoras about 2500 years ago, people have been studying properties of numbers. Today's technology decreases the time and simplifies this work enormously. You can use or adapt the programs below to explore prime numbers and related topics.

PROGRAM: PRIME
: ClrHome
: Input "ENTER INT.>2:", N
: 2→D
: Lbl 1
: If iPart(N/D)=N/D
: Then
: Disp "COMPOSITE"
: Else
: D+1→D
: If D≤√(N)
: Goto 1
: Disp "PRIME"
: End

PROGRAM: FACSUM
: ClrHome
: Input "ENTER INT.>2:", N
: 2→D
: 1→S
: Lbl 1
: If N/D=iPart(N/D)
: S+D+N/D→S
: D+1→D
: If D≤√(N)
: Goto 1
: If D−1=√(N)
: S−√(N)→S
: Disp S

1. **Finding Primes** Enter and run the program PRIME to determine if the following numbers are prime or composite. Then answer the rest of the questions.

   a. 187 _____   **b.** 523 _____

   c. 2027_____   **d.** 5027 _____

   e. Which part, **c** or **d**, took your calculator more time. Explain why this was the case.

   _____

   f. Which line of the program corresponds to the Factor
   Search Theorem?   _____

   g. Does this program do some unnecessary divisions? Explain.

   _____

   _____

2. **Examining Factor Sums** The Pythagoreans were interested in the *factor sum* of a number, the sum of all of its factors that are less than the number itself. If a number's factor sum is equal to the number itself, it is a *perfect number*; if the factor sum is less than the number, it is a *deficient number*; and if the factor sum is greater than the number, the number is an *abundant number*. Six is a perfect number. Until widespread use of computers in the 1950s, only twelve perfect numbers were known.

Enter and run the program FACSUM given on the previous page to find factor sums and answer the following questions.

a. Find a three-digit deficient number. _____

b. Find a three-digit abundant number. _____

c. Try to find a two-digit and a three-digit perfect number. (If you are adept at programming, you might want to revise FACSUM to search for perfect numbers through 999 using a For statement.) _____

d. How could you use this program to determine if a number is prime?

_____

e. Euclid proved that for all integers $n > 1$, if $2^n - 1$ is a prime number, then $2^{n-1}(2^n - 1)$ is a perfect number. Use the FACSUM program to verify this property for some prime number of the form $2^n - 1$.

_____

f. Find the factor sums of 220 and 284. What do you notice? Such pairs of numbers are called *amicable numbers*. More than 900 pairs of amicable numbers have been found.

_____

3. **Using Prime Numbers for Security** Prime numbers play an important role in security codes, not just for national security, but for the transmission of documents and data via networks. Technology leaders are perfecting *public-key encryption*, which would assign to every person a secret private prime number, and a publicly known number which is the product of your prime number and another prime. These numbers would have hundreds of digits handled only by computers so as to keep this simple for individuals. Your private number can "unlock" any transmission sent to you at your public number "address" because a computer can quickly determine if your private number is a factor of the public number. However, and this is the beauty of public-key encryption, even today's fastest computers would take decades or longer to find the two prime factors of a public number 250 digits long, keeping your number safe and secret from others.

Precalculus and Discrete Mathematics © Scott Foresman Addison Wesley

Enter the following program, PRIMEFAC, which gives the prime factors of an integer greater than 2 and stores them in a list, L1. (The program is given in two columns to save space.)

PROGRAM: PRIMEFAC

: ClrHome
: Input "ENTER INT.>2:", N
: 1→dim(L1)
: 1→L1(1)
: 2→D
: Lbl 1
: If iPart (N/D)=N/D and N/D≠1
: Then
: D→L1(dim(L1))
: dim(L1) + 1→dim(L1)
: N/D→N
: Goto 1

: End
: D+1→D
: If D>√(N)
: Goto 2
: Goto 1
: Lbl 2
: N→L1(dim(L1))
: If dim(L1)=1
: Disp N, "IS PRIME."
: If dim(L1)≠1
: Disp "FACTORS IN L1"

a. Run the program to find the prime factors of each number.

5096 _____   4423 _____   271,793 _____

b. Suppose your public number is 6644321 and your private number is 857. How can it be quickly verified without a program that 857 is a factor of 6644321? (This is analogous to your accessing documents meant only for you.)

_____

c. Use PRIMEFAC to find the two prime factors of 6644321. (This is analagous to someone's attempt to steal and use your private number.) How did this task compare to the one in part **b**?

_____

d. Nearly two decades ago it was predicted that it would take computers millions of years to factor a 130-digit public number, but in 1993 a team of 600 people factored a prototypical 129-digit public number in less than a year. What prediction would you make about the security of a private number that is one of two prime factors of a 250-digit public number?

_____

_____

CALCULATOR MASTER 8

Calculator: *Graphics with table capability; GraphExplorer or similar software*

By examining various types of rational functions, you can categorize their local and end behavior.

1. **Describing End Behavior** Consider a rational function r of the type
$$r(x) = \frac{ax + b}{cx^2 + dx + e}.$$

    a. Based on the Theorem for End Behavior of Rational Functions in Lesson 5-5, describe the end behavior of r.

    _____

    b. Would you expect to see a horizontal asymptote to the graph of this type of rational function? If so, state its equation. If not, explain why not.

    _____

2. **Verifying End Behavior** To test your answers to Item **1**, enter
$$f(x) = \frac{2x + 1}{x^2 - 3x - 10} \text{ into your calculator.}$$

    a. Find $f(1000)$ and $f(-1000)$. Record in Table 1 below.

    b. Do your results in the table match your answers to Item **1**? _____

    c. Graph f. In Table 2, record the *local* behavior of f.

    d. Repeat **a** and **c** for $g(x) = \dfrac{2x + 1}{x^2 + 6x + 9}.$

    e. Repeat **a** and **c** for $h(x) = \dfrac{x - 5}{x^2 - 3x - 10}.$

    f. Repeat **a** and **c** for $k(x) = \dfrac{x - 5}{x^2 + 2x + 3}.$

TABLE 1

f		g		h		k	
x	**y = f(x)**	**x**	**y = g(x)**	**x**	**y = h(x)**	**x**	**y = k(x)**
1000		1000		1000		1000	
-1000		-1000		-1000		-1000	

Precalculus and Discrete Mathematics © Scott Foresman Addison Wesley

TABLE 2

Function	Vertical Asymptotes	Oblique Asymptotes	Horizontal Asymptotes	Zeros
f				
g				
h				
k				

3. **Comparing Functions** The four functions have the same end behavior, but they do not have the same local behavior.

   a. Write $f(x)$ in completely factored form by factoring the denominator. How does this form explain the location of vertical asymptotes of f?

   $f(x) =$ _____   _____

   _____

   b. What part of the factored form of $f(x)$ determines the location of its zero(s)? Explain.

   _____

   c. Repeat parts **a** and **b** for $g(x)$, $h(x)$, and $k(x)$. For each function, describe how the factored form helps explain the local behavior.

   $g(x) =$ _____   _____

   _____

   $h(x) =$ _____   _____

   _____

   $k(x) =$ _____   _____

   _____

Precalculus and Discrete Mathematics © Scott Foresman Addison Wesley

4. **Examining Another Type of Rational Function** Now consider a rational function r of the type $r(x) = \dfrac{ax^2 + bx + c}{dx + e}$.

a. Based on the Theorem for End Behavior of Rational Functions, describe the end behavior of r.

_____

b. Would you expect to see a horizontal asymptote to the graph of this type of rational function? If so, state its equation. If not, explain why not.

_____

c. Follow the directions of Questions **2a** and **2c** and Questions **3a** and **3b** for
$q(x) = \dfrac{x^2 - 3x - 10}{x - 4}$ and
$r(x) = \dfrac{x^2 - 6x + 9}{2 - x}$. Record
your results in Tables 3 and 4.

TABLE 3

	q		r	
x	**y = q(x)**	**x**	**y = r(x)**	
1000		1000		
-1000		-1000		

TABLE 4

Function	Vertical Asymptotes	Oblique Asymptotes	Horizontal Asymptotes	Zeros
q				
r				

d. Can the graph of a rational function exhibit both an oblique asymptote and a horizontal asymptote? Explain.

_____

_____

e. Can the graph of a rational function exhibit both an oblique asymptote and a vertical asymptote? Explain.

_____

_____

Precalculus and Discrete Mathematics © Scott Foresman Addison Wesley

CALCULATOR MASTER 9

Calculator: *Graphics; GraphExplorer or similar software*

Rational equations are useful for solving distance-rate-time problems.
Consider the following situation.

Lena is getting in shape for the upcoming Northern Fitness Triathlon that includes a
1.5-km swim, a 40-km bike ride, and a 10-km run. She is trying to break her previous
record of 2:28:35 (2 hours 28 minutes 35 seconds). She is aiming for 2:25:00.

1. **Writing Rational Expressions and Equations** Suppose Lena can complete the swim
   in 24 minutes and the run in 38 minutes. Let x represent Lena's average biking speed.

   a. Write a rational expression in x to represent
   Lena's total time in minutes for the triathlon.   _____

   b. Convert the time 2:25:00 to minutes.   _____

   c. Use parts **a** and **b** to write a rational equation
   Lena can solve to determine her average biking
   speed if she attains her goal of 2:25:00.   _____

2. **Graphing the Equations** Refer to the equation you wrote in **1c**. On your calculator,
   enter the left side of the equation in Y1 and the right side in Y2. Graph in a window
   with $-2 \le x \le 2$ and $-200 \le y \le 200$.

   a. Do you see a solution to the equation from **1c**? Explain.

   _____

   b. Zoom in to find the solution to the nearest ten-thousandth. Tell what the
   solution represents.

   _____

   _____

   c. Lena's best biking speed so far has been .465 km/min.
   By what percent must she increase this speed to reach
   the speed found in part **b**?   _____

3. **Adjusting Lena's Other Speed** Lena's trainer thinks that at best Lena can increase each of her speeds 3%.

   a. Will Lena be able to attain the speed found in **2b**? _____

   b. If her swimming speed increases by 3%, how will this affect her swim time of 24 minutes? (Recall $d = rt.$)

   _____

   c. If her running speed increases by 3%, how will this affect her run time of 38 minutes?

   _____

   d. Change Y1 to reflect these improved swim and run times. What would her biking speed need to be in order to meet her goal? According to her trainer is that attainable? _____

4. **Breaking Other Records** Suppose this year Lena exceeds her goal at the Northern Fitness Triathlon, completing the swim in 23.4 minutes, the bike ride in 84.2 minutes, and the run in 37.3 min. Also, suppose the winning women's time is 2:21:45. Lena hopes to at least tie this time next year.

   a. Lena plans to increase this year's swimming speed by some percent p. She hopes to increase each of this year's biking and running speeds by $2p$. Write a rational expression that gives her total time for the triathlon with these increases in speeds.

   _____

   b. Use this expression to write a rational equation in p that Lena could use to determine the percents by which she must improve her speeds in order to tie the winning time.

   _____

   c. Enter the left side of the equation in Y1 and the right side in Y2. Graph in a window with $-1 \le x \le 1$ and $-20 \le y \le 150$. How many solutions are shown? Which one should you zoom in on?

   _____

   d. Solve for p and interpret the solution.

   _____

Precalculus and Discrete Mathematics © Scott Foresman Addison Wesley

CALCULATOR MASTER 10

Calculator: *Graphics, GraphExplorer or similar software*

You have seen how graphing can help you "test out" suspected identities, but that ultimately you must use proof to establish that an equation is an identity.

1. **Conjecturing Identities** Now it's your turn to write some identities of your own. Choose the left side of your possible identity from column I below and the right side from column II. Then use an automatic grapher to test out your conjecture.

Twenty possible identities can be formed. See if you can find them all.

COLUMN I	COLUMN II
$\cos\left(x + \frac{\pi}{2}\right)$	$\sin\left(x + \frac{\pi}{2}\right)$
$\cos\left(x - \frac{\pi}{2}\right)$	$\sin\left(x - \frac{\pi}{2}\right)$
$\cos\left(x + \pi\right)$	$\sin\left(x + \pi\right)$
$\cos\left(x - \pi\right)$	$\sin\left(x - \pi\right)$
$\cos\left(x + 2\pi\right)$	$\sin\left(x + 2\pi\right)$
$\cos\left(\frac{\pi}{2} - x\right)$	$\sin\left(\frac{\pi}{2} - x\right)$
$\cos\left(\pi - x\right)$	$\sin\left(\pi - x\right)$
$\cos\left(\frac{3\pi}{2} - x\right)$	$\sin\left(\frac{3\pi}{2} - x\right)$
$\cos\left(2\pi - x\right)$	$\sin\left(x - 2\pi\right)$

(1) _____ (2) _____

(3) _____ (4) _____

(5) _____ (6) _____

(7) _____ (8) _____

(9) _____ (10) _____

(11) _____ (12) _____

(13) _____ (14) _____

(15) _____ (16) _____

(17) _____ (18) _____

(19) _____ (20) _____

2.   Proving Identities   Write proofs for three of the identities you conjectured.

(1) _____

(2) _____

(3) _____

CALCULATOR MASTER 11

Calculator: *Programmable*

The following program generates the first 100 terms of the sequence defined by the recurrence relation $a_{k+1} = a_k^2 + c$. Both c, a constant, and a_1, the first term, are input by the user.

```
PROGRAM: SIMPSEQ
    : ClrHome
    : Input "ENTER C:", C
    : Input "1ST TERM:", T
    : For(N,1,100,1)
    : N→dim(L1)
    : T→L1(N)
    : T^2+C→T
    : End
    : Disp "SERIES IN L1"
```

1. **Analyzing the Sequence for $c = 0$**   Consider the sequence defined by
$$\begin{cases} a_1 \\ a_{k+1} = a_k{}^2. \end{cases}$$

   a. Run the program. You will get an overflow message. What does that mean?

   _____

   b. What is $\lim\limits_{n\to\infty} a_n$?   _____

   c. Rerun the program with $a_1 = \frac{1}{2}$ and $c = 0$. What is $\lim\limits_{n\to\infty} a_n$?_____

   d. Use the program to help complete the table below.

$c = 0$	a_1	2	$\frac{1}{2}$	1	.99	1.01	-1	-1.01	0	-.7
	$\lim\limits_{n\to\infty} a_n$									

   e. Describe how $\lim\limits_{n\to\infty} a_n$ depends on a_1 when $c = 0$.

   _____

   f. What value(s) of a_1 produce a sequence of terms all equal to a_1 itself? Any such value is called a **fixed point** of the recurrence relation.   _____

2. **Determining Fixed Points** Consider the sequence defined using the recurrence relation $a_{k+1} = a_k^2 - 6$.

   a. To find the fixed points, solve the equation $x = x^2 - 6$. _____

   b. Use the program, or mentally check that when a_1 is equal to any value you found in part **a**, every term of the sequence is equal to a_1.

3. **Determining Fixed Points in Another Sequence** Consider the sequence defined using the recurrence relation $a_{k+1} = a_k^2 - \frac{1}{2}$.

   a. Find the exact values of the two fixed points.
   Also give decimal approximations. _____

   b. Use the program to check one of your fixed points. If you got an overflow message, why do you think this happened? You can still check your fixed points by editing your program to generate just the first 10 or 20 terms.

   _____

   c. Use the program to help complete the table below.

		greater fixed point ⇓			lesser fixed point ⇓		
$c = -\frac{1}{2}$	a_1	2		1	.5		-1	-2
	$\lim\limits_{n\to\infty} a_n$							

   d. Now "zoom in" and explore $\lim\limits_{n\to\infty} a_n$ for values of a_1 that are very slightly less than or very slightly greater than the absolute value of the fixed points. Remember, if you get an overflow message, edit your program to generate fewer terms. Then describe the results.

$c = -\frac{1}{2}$	a_1						
	$\lim\limits_{n\to\infty} a_n$						

   _____

4. **Examining Periodic Points** Explore the sequence defined by the recurrence relation $a_{k+1} = a_k^2 - 1$.

   a. Find the fixed points of the recurrence relation. _____

Precalculus and Discrete Mathematics © Scott Foresman Addison Wesley

b. Describe the behavior of the sequence for the given values of a_1.

		greater fixed point ⇓					lesser fixed point ⇓		
$c = -1$	a_1	2		.5	0	-.5		-1	-2
	behavior								

c. The numbers 0 and -1 are called **periodic points of this recurrence relation** with period 2. Why is this so?

_____

5. **Examining Periodic Points in Another Sequence**   Do a similar analysis for $a_{k+1} = a_k^2 - 1.3$.

a. Using the fixed points and a variety of other points for a_1, complete the following table.

$c = -1.3$	a_1								
	behavior								

b. What do the periodic points appear to be?   _____

c. What is the period?   _____

6. **Observing Chaos**   Explore $a_{k+1} = a_k^2 - 2$.

a. Using the fixed points and a variety of other points for a_1, complete another table for at least 12 values of a_1.

b. Does this sequence seem to have any periodic points?   _____

(The behavior of this recurrence relation for certain values of a_1 is called **chaotic**.)

CALCULATOR MASTER 12

Calculator: *Graphics, GraphExplorer or similar software*

By studying the graphs of various polar equations, you can see the relationships between the equations and some characteristics of the graphs.

1. **Exploring Rose Curves**   In Lesson 8-5 you learned that rose curves are polar graphs of equations of the form $r = a \cos n\theta$, for $a > 0$ and n a positive integer or $r = a \sin n\theta$, for $a > 0$ and n a positive integer.

   a. Explain what characteristics of the curve are determined by n and by a.

   _____

   _____

   Set your automatic grapher to polar mode. Graph each pair of equations for $0 \le \theta \le 2\pi$.

   i. $r = \cos 2\theta$ and $r = \sin 2\theta$ **ii.** $r = \cos 3\theta$ and $r = \sin 3\theta$

   iii. $r = \cos 4\theta$ and $r = \sin 4\theta$ **iv.** $r = \cos 5\theta$ and $r = \sin 5\theta$

   b. With respect to the axes, what is the difference between the graph of $r = \cos 3\theta$ and that of $r = \sin 3\theta$?

   _____

   c. With respect to the axes, what is the difference between the graph of $r = \cos 4\theta$ and that of $r = \sin 4\theta$?

   _____

   d. With respect to the axes, what is the difference between the graph of $r = \cos n\theta$ and that of $r = \sin n\theta$?

   _____

   _____

Precalculus and Discrete Mathematics © Scott Foresman Addison Wesley

2. **Extending the Exploration**   Examine what happens when θ is replaced with $\theta - \frac{\pi}{k}$.

 a. Graph $r = \sin 2\theta$ and $r = \sin 2\left(\theta - \frac{\pi}{4}\right)$. What do you notice about the two graphs?

 _____

 b. Graph $r = \sin 2\theta$ and $r = \sin 2\left(\theta - \frac{\pi}{8}\right)$. Compare the two graphs.

 _____

 c. How does the graph of $r = \sin 2\theta$ compare to that of $r = \sin 2\left(\theta - \frac{\pi}{k}\right)$?

 _____

3. **Exploring Lemniscate Curves**   The polar graph of $r^2 = a^2 \cos 2\theta$, where a is a real number, is called a *lemniscate*.

 a. Consider $r^2 = \cos 2\theta$. Solve for r and graph the equation over $0 \le \theta \le 2\pi$. You will need to graph both the positive and negative square roots. Describe the graph.

 _____

 b. Graph $r^2 = 4 \cos 2\theta$ and $r^2 = 9 \cos 2\theta$. What affect does a have on the graph of $r^2 = a^2 \cos 2\theta$?

 _____

 c. Experiment to determine an equation containing the sine function that has the same polar graph as $r^2 = \cos 2\theta$.

 _____

 d. Suppose the graph of $r^2 = \cos 2\theta$ is rotated about the pole through an angle of magnitude $\frac{\pi}{4}$. Find an equation for the image.

 _____

CALCULATOR MASTER 13

Calculator: *Programmable*

You can use both algebra and calculator programs to determine equations for secant lines through two points on the graph of a function. In turn, the slope of secant lines can help us to conjecture the slope of the tangent line to a curve at a particular point $(x, f(x))$, otherwise known as the *instantaneous rate of change* or the *derivative* at that point.

1. **Using Algebra**   Consider the function f with $f(x) = x^2 - 4x$. Use the familiar algebraic method below to find the slope of the secant line through $(x, f(x))$ and $(x + \Delta x, f(x + \Delta x))$ when $x = 3$ and $\Delta x = 2$.

   a. Find the two points on the curve. _____

   b. Find the slope m of the line containing these two points. _____

   c. Substitute the slope and one of the points into slope-intercept form $y = mx + b$ to solve for the y-intercept b. Then write an equation for the secant line.

   _____

2. **Using a Program**   The process in Question **1** is not terribly difficult, but performing it repeatedly would be tedious. The following program will compute the slope and y-intercept of the secant line through $(x, f(x))$ and $(x + \Delta x, f(x + \Delta x))$ for any function f.

   PROGRAM: SLOPESEC
     :ClrHome
     :Input "ENTER X:",X
     :Input "DELTA X:",D
     :(Y₁(X+D) −Y₁(X))/D→S
     :Disp "SLOPE:",S
     :Y₁(X+D) −S(X+D)→B
     :Disp "Y INT:",B

   a. Enter the program or an equivalent into your calculator. _____

   b. To run the program for the function of Item **1**, first enter $Y_1 = x^2 - 4x$. Then use the output to complete the following table. (Note that $x = 3$ for the entire table, but Δx changes.)

Precalculus and Discrete Mathematics © Scott Foresman Addison Wesley

Secant line through (3, $f(3)$) and (3 + Δx, $f(3 + \Delta x)$); $f(x) = x^2 - 4x$			
Δx	Slope	y-intercept	Equation
2			
1			
0.5			
0.1			
0.01			
-0.01			
-0.1			
-0.5			
-1			
-2			

3. **Examining the Graphs** Graph f and the secant lines from the table for $\Delta x = 1, 0.5$, and 0.1 on your calculator in the window $0 \leq x \leq 5$ and $-5 \leq y \leq 2$.

   a. Do any of the secant lines look tangent to the graph of f? If yes, which one(s)?

   _____

   b. Zoom in on the point (3, -3). Some calculators allow you to draw a box around the area you want to see more closely. Can you verify visually that all three lines are secant lines? If not, which one(s) still look tangent?

   _____

   c. Remove the graphs of the secant lines from part **a**. Then graph f and the secant lines from the table for $\Delta x = -1, -0.5$, and -0.1 on your calculator in the window $0 \leq x \leq 5$ and $-5 \leq y \leq 2$. Which, if any, of the secant lines look tangent to the graph of f?

   _____

4. **Making a Conjecture** Examine the second column of your table.

   a. Conjecture the value of $\lim\limits_{x \to 0} \dfrac{f(3 + \Delta x) - f(3)}{\Delta x}$. _____

b. Use the method of Lesson 9-2 to prove your conjecture in part **a.**

_____

_____

c. What is the slope of the tangent line to the graph
of f at $x = 3$?　　　　　　　　　　_____

d. Write an equation in slope-intercept form for the
tangent line to the graph of f at $x = 3$.　　_____

e. Graph the tangent line to f at $x = 3$ along with f without any secant lines.

f. Find $f'(3)$.　　　　　　　　　　_____

5. **Examining Another Function**　Change the function in Y1 to $f(x) = \frac{1}{2}x^2 - 4x$.

a. Run SLOPESEC in order to conjecture the value

　　of $\lim\limits_{x \to 0} \dfrac{f(2 + \Delta x) - f(2)}{\Delta x}$.　　　　_____

b. Prove your conjecture from part **a.**

_____

_____

c. Use the program to conjecture the slope of the tangent line to the graph of f at
$x = 4$. Then find an equation for this line. Graph $f(x)$ along with the line in the
window $0 \le x \le 10$ and $-10 \le y \le 2$.

_____

d. Find an equation for the tangent line to the graph
of f at $x = 6$.　　　　　　　　　_____

e. Find a point P on the graph of f such that the slope of the tangent line to the graph
of f at P is 6. Then find an equation for the tangent line to the graph at P.

_____

f. Graph f along with the line from part **e** in the window $0 \le x \le 15$ and
$-15 \le y \le 30$. Zoom in on the point P to verify visually that the line is
tangent to the curve.

Precalculus and Discrete Mathematics © Scott Foresman Addison Wesley

CALCULATOR MASTER 14

Calculator: *Programmable*

In some lotteries, a ticket buyer has the choice of picking the numbers personally or letting the computer "pick" them. The chances that a computer picks the winning numbers depends on how many numbers there are and the choices available for each number. Consider those lotteries in which the ticket numbers, such as 24 18 5, must match the winning numbers *in order*. Recall that we call such an ordered set of numbers a *string*.

The program below (given in two columns to save space) simulates a computer generating random lottery tickets and comparing these tickets to the winning numbers. The program counts how many tickets it takes to produce a winner. When you use the program, you will be asked the length of the string (how many numbers are in the string) and how many choices are available for each number. Then you will also be asked what the winning numbers are, and you will need to enter them in order, one at a time. The computer keeps picking random strings of lottery numbers until a match to the winning string is found. (This program does not allow the computer to "remember" which strings it has already tried.)

```
PROGRAM: PICKWIN
  : Input "LENGTH:", L           : Lbl A
  : Input "CHOICES:", C          : T+1→T
  : L→dim(L1)                    : For (N,1,L,1)
  : For(N,1,L,1)                 : If iPart(rand*C)≠L1(N)
  : Input "WINNING NO.:",E       : Goto A
  : E→L1(N)                      : End
  : End                         : Disp "TICKETS:",T
  : 0→T
```

1. **Entering and Running the Program**   Consider a 2-number lottery (length = 2), each number from 0 to 5 (choices = 6). Make up the winning ticket. (If you prefer to have the calculator randomly select each winning number, enter iPart(rand*6) and then press Enter. Press Enter again for the second number.) Enter the program PICKWIN.

   a. How many such 2-number strings are possible?   _____

   b. Run PICKWIN five times and record the average
   number of tickets required to produce the winner.   _____

2. **Changing the Restrictions**   Repeat the process in Item **1** for strings of length *l*, with *c* choices for each number, as given in the table on the next page. Then give the number of possible strings *p* and the average number of tickets *t* from five trials.

   To save time, try to work with four other students, each with their own calculator. Each needs to run the program just once for each type of string.

Helpful Hint: If you find your calculator gives a memory error for any of these strings, replace the last 5 lines of the program with those at the right. They seem to use less memory.

```
: 0→Z
: For (N,1,L,1)
: Z+abs(L1(N)–iPart(rand*C))→Z
: End
: If Z≠0
: Goto A
: Disp "TICKETS:",T
```

a.

l	*c*	*p*	*t*
2	10		
2	20		
2	30		

b. What is the relationship between *p* and *t*? _____

c. What is the relationship between *c* and *p*? _____

d. What happens if you double *c*? _____

e. What happens if you triple *c*? _____

3. **Exploring 3-Number Lotteries** Run PICKWIN to complete the table below for 3-number strings.

a.

l	*c*	*p*	*t*
3	6		
3	10		
3	20		
3	30		

b. How do your answers to parts **b–e** of Item **2** change in this case?

_____

_____

Precalculus and Discrete Mathematics © Scott Foresman Addison Wesley

4. **Relating Possible Strings to Length and Choices** Find the values of p to complete the table below.

a.

l	p, when $c = 6$	p, when $c = 10$	p, when $c = 20$	p, when $c = 30$	p, when $c = 40$
2					
3					
4					
5					
6					

b. For a fixed value of c, give an equation relating c, l, and p. _____

c. Study your equation in part **b**. Doubling l has the same effect on p as doing what to c? _____

d. Tripling l has the same effect on p as doing what to c? _____

e. Consider a 3-number lottery with 10 choices per number. Verify that the following changes produce the same increase in possible strings. (This relates to part **c**.)
   • changing to a 6-number lottery, but keeping the choices per number the same
   • changing the choices per number to 100, but keeping the lottery 3 numbers

_____

_____

5. **Choosing Lotteries** Choose the lottery with the better chances for winning and justify your answer.

a. Lottery A: 3 numbers, 0 through 39 for each number

Lottery B: 4 numbers, 0 through 19 for each number

_____

b. Lottery A: 6 numbers, 0 through 5 for each number

Lottery B: 4 numbers, 0 through 9 for each number

_____

Precalculus and Discrete Mathematics © Scott Foresman Addison Wesley

CALCULATOR MASTER 15

Calculator: *Programmable*

The program below simulates coin-tossing experiments with a fair coin. In the program, E represents the total number of experiments performed, T represents the number of tosses per experiment, K represents the number of heads that resulted in each experiment, and H represents the total number of heads obtained from all tosses in all experiments. (The program is presented in two columns to save space.)

```
PROGRAM: COIN
  : ClrHome                           : ClrHome
  : Input "NUM OF EXPTS:", E          : Disp "EXPT NUM",S,
  : Input "TOSSES PER EXPT:",T          "HAD",K,"HEADS"
  : 0→H                               : Pause
  : For(S,1,E,1)                      : ClrHome
  : 0→K                               : H+K→H
  : For(Q,1,T,1)                      : End
  : iPart(2*rand)+K→K                 : Disp "THERE WERE", H,
  : End                                 "HEADS OUT OF",T*E,"TOSSES"
```

1. **Running the Program**   Run the program with 1 experiment ($E = 1$) and 20 tosses ($T = 20$.) Remember to press Enter after the pause in the program.

   a. How many tosses come up heads?   _____

   b. What is the expected number of heads?   _____

   c. Use the program to complete the table below for one experiment and the given number of tosses. Each time, calculate the relative frequency of heads.

Number of Tosses, T	Number of Heads, H	Relative Frequency, $R = \dfrac{H}{T}$
10		
20		
50		
100		
200		

Precalculus and Discrete Mathematics © Scott Foresman Addison Wesley

d. What appears to be the limit of R as T approaches infinity? _____

2. Simulating Several Experiments Now simulate several experiments with 6 tosses per experiment.

a. What fraction of the total number of experiments do you predict will produce 3 heads? 2 heads?

_____

b. Use the program to complete the table for 10 experiments, 6 tosses per experiment. As you run the program, use tally marks in the table below to record how many experiments produce 0 heads, 1 head, 2 heads, and so on. Then calculate the relative frequencies of each outcome.

10 Experiments		
Number of Heads, K, per Experiment	Number of Experiments, N Producing K Heads	Relative Frequency, $R = \dfrac{N}{10}$
0		
1		
2		
3		
4		
5		
6		

c. Repeat part **b** for $E = 20$ and $T = 6$. Then repeat for $E = 50$ and $T = 6$. Complete the tables below.

20 Experiments		
K	**N**	$R = \dfrac{N}{10}$
0		
1		
2		
3		
4		
5		
6		

50 Experiments		
K	**N**	$R = \dfrac{N}{10}$
0		
1		
2		
3		
4		
5		
6		

3. **Comparing to the Binomial Probability**   Refer to the procedure for calculating binomial probabilities in Lesson 10-6.

a. Calculate each probability $P(K)$ for obtaining K heads out of 6 tosses. Round to the nearest hundredth. Record your results in the table below.

K	**P(K)**
0	
1	
2	
3	
4	
5	
6	

b. How well do the relative frequencies from your experiments match the binomial probabilities?

_____

_____

_____

c. Pool your data from **2c** with others in your class. Calculate the relative frequencies of K heads out of 6. Do you find that these values match the probabilities more closely than the relative frequencies determined for each individual set of 50 experiments?

_____

Precalculus and Discrete Mathematics © Scott Foresman Addison Wesley

Name _____

CALCULATOR MASTER 16

Calculator: *Graphics with matrix capability*

When demographers study the U.S. population, they sometimes divide the country into four major regions: the Northeast, the Midwest, the South, and the West.

1. **Representing Population Trends with Matrices** Over time there is a flow of people moving from one region to another. During 1995, this movement between regions was as follows:

   From the Northeast, .048% of the population moved to the Midwest, .139% moved to the South, and .069% moved to the West.

   From the Midwest, .045% of the population moved to the Northeast, .171% moved to the South, and .079% moved to the West.

   From the South, .096% of the population moved to the Northeast, .183% moved to the Midwest, and .152% moved to the West.

   From the West, .027% of the population moved to the Northeast, .089% moved to the Midwest, and .178% moved to the South.

   a. Assume there are no other changes in population. Convert these percents to decimals and write a 4×4 *transition matrix T* which represents these population shifts. Caution: Be sure to organize the information so that the sum of each row is 1.

$$T = \quad \begin{matrix} & N & M & S & W \\ N \\ M \\ S \\ W \end{matrix} \begin{bmatrix} & & & \\ & & & \\ & & & \\ & & & \end{bmatrix}$$

   b. At the beginning of 1995, 19.6% of the U.S. population lived in the Northeast, 23.5% lived in the Midwest, 35.0% lived in the South, and 21.9% lived in the West. Write a 1×4 *population matrix P* which stores this information.

$$P = \quad \begin{matrix} N & M & S & W \\ \begin{bmatrix} & & & \end{bmatrix} \end{matrix}$$

Precalculus and Discrete Mathematics © Scott Foresman Addison Wesley

c. Set the number of decimal places your calculator displays to 5. Enter both matrices into your calculator. Use matrix multiplication $P \cdot T$ to find the percent of population residing in each region at the beginning of 1996. Record these percents to the nearest hundredth of a percent.

North _____%   Midwest _____%   South _____%   West _____%

d. Assuming that the population shift described above continues indefinitely, give the percent in each region at the beginning of 2000, 2010, and 2020. To perform repeated matrix multiplication swiftly on your calculator, repeat your calculation in part **c.** Then multiply this result by matrix T, and continue to press Enter. This process is called *iteration*. Be sure to keep track of the year as you iterate and to record the data required in the following table.

Region	2000	2010	2020
Northeast			
Midwest			
South			
West			

2. Examining Powers of the Transition Matrix Recall from Lesson 11-6 that T is a stochastic matrix. It is usually easier to multiply by powers of T than to keep track of iterations.

a. To find the percent of the population in each region of the U.S. at the beginning of 2000, the entries of T^5 can be multiplied by the 1995 percentages given in P since 2000 is 5 years after 1995. Use your calculator to find T^5.

$$T^5 = \begin{bmatrix} & & & \end{bmatrix}$$

b. Compute $P \cdot T^5$ to find the population percentages for 2000. Do they agree with your answer to **1d**? Similarly, you can multiply $P \cdot T^{15}$ and $P \cdot T^{25}$ to check your other figures. _____

Precalculus and Discrete Mathematics © Scott Foresman Addison Wesley

For very large values of k, T^k is a stochastic matrix with nearly identical rows. Sometimes, as in the lesson, k can be as small as 10 to produce such a stochastic matrix. This means that T^{10} can be used to predict long-term trends. But this is not always the case. Sometimes k must be much, much larger to produce a stochastic matrix with nearly identical rows.

c. Explore very large powers of T. Use powering on your calculator to find A^{100}. Then raise this result to the 2nd power (for T^{200}), the 10th power (for T^{1000}), and so on. Find a value of k for which the rows of T^k appear to be identical.

$$k = \underline{\qquad} \qquad T^k = \begin{bmatrix} & & & \\ & & & \\ & & & \\ & & & \end{bmatrix}$$

d. Multiply $P \cdot T^k$ and explain the results in terms of long-term trends.

_____

_____

e. Suppose the population percentages in 1995 had been 10% in the Northeast, 20% in the Midwest, 30% in the South, and 40% in the West. Adjust your matrix P accordingly and, using the value of k you gave in **c**, determine what will the population distriution be after k years.

_____

f. If the population percentages in 1995 had been 50% in the Northeast, 30% in the Midwest, 10% in the South, and 10% in the West, what will happen after k years?

_____

g. If there are no other factors affecting population distribution, describe the population distribution of the United States after k years. For the size of k you determined, do you think this long-term prediction is realistic? Explain.

_____

_____

3. **Exploring Other Population Trends**   Suppose that in a particular metropolitan area in 1998, 42% of the population lived within the city limits and 58% lived in surrounding suburbs. Suppose also that each year 2.3% of those living in the city move to the suburbs, and 1.1% of those in the suburbs move into the city.

a. Write a 1×2 matrix to represent the population matrix and a 2×2 matrix to represent the transition matrix.

$$P = \begin{matrix} \text{C} & \text{S} \\ \left[\right] \end{matrix} \qquad T = \begin{matrix} & \text{C} & \text{S} \\ \begin{matrix}\text{C}\\\text{S}\end{matrix} & \left[\right] \end{matrix}$$

b. According to the analysis in Item **2**, how can the long-term population percentages be determined if the trends described above continue indefinitely? Are both matrices needed to make this determination?

_____

_____

c. Assuming the trends continue indefinitely, what are the percentages of the population in each area after many, many years?

City _____%   Suburbs _____%

Precalculus and Discrete Mathematics © Scott Foresman Addison Wesley

CALCULATOR MASTER 17

Calculator: *Graphics*

Consider the line in 2-space defined by the parametric equations $\begin{cases} x = -2 + 3t \\ y = 3 + t \end{cases}$.

This line has a vector equation $(x, y) = (-2, 3) + t(3, 1)$.

1. **Graphing the Line** We know that this line contains point $P = (-2, 3)$ and is parallel to the vector $\vec{v} = (3, 1)$.

   a. If Q_t represents any point on the line, then the line's vector equation can be written as follows. $\overrightarrow{PQ} = t\vec{v} = t$ _____

   b. Set your calculator to parametric mode and enter the parametric equations above. Set the window as follows:

Tmin = 0	Xmin = -10	Ymin = -2
Tmax = 3	Xmax = 10	Ymax = 10
Tstep = 1	Xscl = 1	Yscl = 1

   Graph your equations. What do you notice? _____

   c. To understand the results of part **b**, complete the table below and plot each point Q_t on the grid.

Point Q_t	t	x	y
Q_0	0		
Q_1	1		
Q_2	2		
Q_3	3		

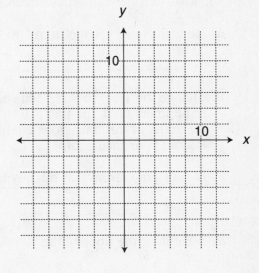

d. The work can be sped up by using a translation to locate each point Q_{t+1} from the previous point Q_t. Describe this translation and tell how it is related to $\vec{v}$.

_____

_____

e. Use the translation in part **d** to plot Q_4.
What are its coordinates? _____

f. Complete the table at right for negative values of t and graph each point Q_t on the grid in part **c**.

Point	t	x	y
Q_{-1}	-1		
Q_{-2}	-2		
Q_{-3}	-3		

g. How would you modify the T-values in the window from part **b** so that you will see a "line" and not a segment? Implement your changes.

_____

h. Change your window so that $-20 \le x \le 20$. Did your modification really produce a line? Explain.

_____

2. Adjusting the Tstep   Change your calculator to dot mode and regraph, using the window from Item **1g**. Your screen should match the graph you plotted by hand.

a. Now change the Tstep from 1 to 0.5. What do you notice in the graph?

_____

b. Change the Tstep to 0.2. Then change it to 0.1.
Experiment until you find a Tstep that makes
the graph of the "line" look continuous.
Record your final choice. _____

c. Is your graph from part **b** really continuous? Explain.

_____

d. What does the slope of the "line" appear to be? _____

Precalculus and Discrete Mathematics © Scott Foresman Addison Wesley

e. How is the slope related to the vector $\vec{v} = (3, 1)$?   _____

f. Solve the first parametric equation for t. Substitute
the result in the second parametric equation in order
to obtain an equation for y in terms of x.   _____

g. According to this equation, what is the slope of the line? _____

3. **Examining Another Line**   Now consider the line with parametric equations
$$\begin{cases} x = 4 - 3t \\ y = \text{-}2 + 2t \end{cases}$$

a. The line contains the point $P = (\underline{\quad}, \underline{\quad})$
and is parallel to the vector $\vec{v} = (\underline{\quad}, \underline{\quad})$.

b. Graph these equations on your calculator, using a Tstep that appears to
"fill in" the line.

c. If Q_k is a point on the line, describe the translation mapping Q_k onto Q_{k+1} and
relate it to $\vec{v}$.

_____

d. Find an equation in the form $y = mx + b$ for this line.
Give the slope of the line and relate it to $\vec{v}$.   _____

4. **Making Generalizations**   Let ℓ be the line through $P = (x_0, y_0)$, and parallel to
$\vec{v} = (v_1, v_2)$.

a. Give parametric equations for ℓ.   _____

b. If Q_k is a point on ℓ, describe the translation mapping Q_k onto Q_{k+1}.

_____

c. Use the equations from part **a** to find an equation in
the form $y = mx + b$ for ℓ. Then give the slope of ℓ.   _____

CALCULATOR MASTER 18

Calculator: *Programmable*

The area between the graph of a function f and the x-axis from a to b is the definite integral, $\int_a^b f(x)\,dx$. Its value is between the lower and upper Riemann sums. As the number of subintervals increases, these sums become better and better approximations of the definite integral. Is it possible to determine just how close these approximations are?

1. **Interpreting the Sums** The program RIEMANN below gives both the upper and lower Riemann sums for a function entered in Y_1 over the interval from a to b for n subintervals. Enter the program. (It is shown in two columns to save space.)

PROGRAM: RIEMANN
```
: ClrHome                           : Y1*W→P
: Input "LEFT ENDPT:",A             : L+P→L
: Input "RIGHT ENDPT:",B            : R+P→R
: Input "SUBINTERVALS:",N           : End
: (B–A)/N→W                         : X+W→X
: 0→R                               : R+Y1*W→R
: A→X                               : Disp "LOWER SUM:",min(L,R)
: Y1*W→L                            : Disp "UPPER SUM:",max(L,R)
: FOR (I,1,N–1,1)
: X+W→X
```

a. Enter the function $f(x) = x^2 + 2$ into Y_1. Run the program for the interval 0 to 3 with six subintervals. Give the upper and lower Riemann sums.

b. Graph the function over the specified interval. Draw the rectangles that yield the lower Riemann sum. Shade these rectangles. On the same set of axes, draw the rectangles that yield the upper Riemann sum.

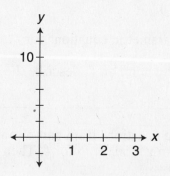

The difference between each sum and $\int_a^b f(x)\,dx$ is the error for that sum. Since $\int_a^b f(x)\,dx$ must be between the lower and upper Riemann sums, the error must be no greater than the difference between the two sums. This difference is therefore an **error bound** for each sum.

c. On your sketch in part **b** use a different color to shade the little rectangles whose total area represents this error bound.

d. If you stacked the rectangles in part **c** on top of each other, what would be the height, width, and area of the resulting rectangle?

_____

2. **Finding a Formula for the Error Bound**   Refer to the function and interval in Question **1**.

a. Use the program to help complete the table below.

Number n of subintervals	Lower Riemann sum	Upper Riemann sum	Error bound, E
6			
10			
50			
100			
1000			

b. Try to find a formula that relates E to n.
(Hint: What is $E \cdot n$?)   _____

c. Refer to Question **1d**. The same stacking procedure for larger values of n results in a rectangle whose area is the error bound for that value of n. Its height, 9, stays constant. Its width is the width of the subinterval, $\dfrac{b-a}{n} = \dfrac{3}{n}$. Give the area of this rectangle in terms of *n*.

_____

d. Verify that the area in part **c** matches the error bound in your table for $n = 100$.

_____

3. Minimizing the Error Bound   Consider the function f with $f(x) = \cos\frac{x}{2}$.

a. Graph the function over the interval $0 \le x \le \pi$

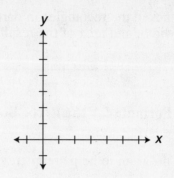

b. Use RIEMANN to help complete the table below. Remember to enter the function in Y1 before you run the program.

Number n of subintervals	Lower Riemann sum	Upper Riemann sum	Error bound, E
10			
50			
100			
1000			

c. Find a formula that relates E to n.   _____

d. Using the same stacking procedure you used earlier, give the height of the rectangle that represents the error bound. You might find this easier to determine if you sketch the appropriate rectangles as in Question **2c** using just a few subintervals.

_____

e. Give the width of the rectangle in terms of n. Then give the area of the rectangle in terms of n.

_____

f. Verify that the area in part **e** matches the error bound in your table for $n = 100$.

_____

g. Use the formula to find n such that the error bound is less than .0001. Then use RIEMANN to verify that your choice of n works.

_____

Precalculus and Discrete Mathematics © Scott Foresman Addison Wesley

CALCULATOR MASTER 19

Calculator: *Programmable*

This investigation explores the areas of rose curves you studied in Chapter 8.

1. **Making Predications** Shown at the right is the graph of the rose curve with equation $r = \sin 2\theta$ along with the graph of $r = 1$, the unit circle. The interior of the rose curve has been shaded.

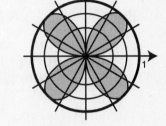

   a. What is the area of the unit circle? _____

   b. What do you think is the total area of all four petals in the rose curve? _____

2. **Slicing the Petal** Imagine slicing a petal as one might slice up a pie, by rotating the slicing edge about the origin. The resulting pieces can be approximated by sectors of a circle. Recall that the area of a sector of a circle with radius r and central angle θ is $\frac{1}{2}r^2\theta$, where θ is in radians.

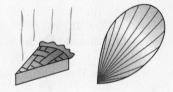

   a. What interval for θ is used to draw the petal in the first quadrant? _____

   Suppose this petal is sliced by dividing the interval into n equal subintervals.

   b. What is the measure of the central angle of each slice? _____

   c. Let θ_1 be the direction of the first cut, θ_2 the direction of the second cut, and so on. Give the measure of each direction in terms of π and n.

   θ_1 _____ θ_2 _____ θ_3 _____ θ_i _____

   The area of the ith slice could be approximated by the area of a sector with central angle $\frac{\pi}{2n}$ and radius r_i, where $r_i = \sin 2\theta_i$.

   d. What is the area of this sector? _____

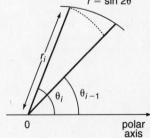

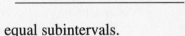

Precalculus and Discrete Mathematics © Scott Foresman Addison Wesley

e. The sum of the areas of all *n* sectors approximates the area of the rose petal. Express this sum using summation notation and your answer to part **d.** _____

3. **Using a Program**   The following program uses the techniques in Item **2** to approximate the area of the petal. To use the program, you must first enter $Y_1 = \sin(2\theta)$. Make sure to use θ in Y_1 and not *x*. (The program is given in two columns to save space.)

PROGRAM: PTLAREA

```
: ClrHome                        : FOR (I,1,N,1)
: Input "LEFT ENDPT:",A          : A+I*W→θ
: Input "RIGHT ENDPT:",B         : S+Y₁^2/2*W→S
: Input "SUBINTERVALS:",N        : End
: (B–A)/N→W                      : Disp "AREA:",S
: 0→S
```

Enter and run the program for the interval $0 \le \theta \le \frac{\pi}{2}$. Try *n* = 10, then *n* = 200, and then *n* = 1000.

a. Does the value of *n* appear to affect the output? (Caution: These results do not hold for all graphs.) _____

b. Give the approximate area of the petal. _____

c. Give the approximate area of all four petals. _____

d. Express the answer to part **c** in terms of π. Then comment on how this quantity compares to your prediction in Item **1b**.

_____

4. **Changing the Rose Curve**   Enter $Y_1 = \sin(4\theta)$ and graph this equation.

a. How many petals are there? _____

b. What interval of θ gives rise to the first petal? _____

c. Run the program for this rose curve. Then give the approximate total area of all the petals. _____

d. Now enter and graph $Y_1 = \sin(6\theta)$. Repeat parts **a–c**.

_____

NOTE: In addition to the answers shown, please see students' printouts of diagrams, graphs, or tables.

Computer Master 1

1. **c.** Russo, O'Hare, Krutz, Chin, Lyon
   d. When either one or both of these statements are true: $B2 \geq 28$; $C2+D2 \geq 1300$
   e. It prints "honors" in the cell.
2. **b.** Lyon
   c. When both of these statements are true: $B2 \geq 28$; $C2+D2 \geq 1300$
   d. It prints "regular" in the cell.
3. **a.** Sample:
   =IF(AND(OR(B2>=28, C2+D2>=1250),E2>=90), "honors", "regular")
   b. O'Hare, Herrera, Krutz, Chin

Computer Master 2

1–2. Drawings will vary.

Computer Master 3

2. **a.** circle centered at $(0, 0)$ with radius 2
   b. $x^2 = 4 \cos^2 t$ and $y^2 = 4 \sin^2 t$. So $x^2 + y^2 = 4\cos^2 t + 4\sin^2 t = 4(\cos^2 t + \sin^2 t) = 4(1) = 4$. $x^2 + y^2 = 4$ is a circle centered at $(0, 0)$ with radius 2.
   c. Predictions will vary.
   d. circle centered at $(0, 0)$ with radius $|a|$.
3. **a.** ellipse centered at $(0, 0)$ with vertical major axis 6 and minor axis 4
   b. $\frac{x}{2} = \cos t$ and $\frac{y}{3} = \sin t$.
   So $\left(\frac{x}{2}\right)^2 + \left(\frac{y}{3}\right)^2 = \cos^2 t + \sin^2 t = 1$. $\left(\frac{x}{2}\right)^2 + \left(\frac{y}{3}\right)^2 = 1$ is an ellipse centered at $(0, 0)$ with vertical major axis 6 and minor axis 4.
   c. Predictions will vary.

d. $\frac{x+1}{4} = \cos t$ and $\frac{y-2}{3} = \sin t$. So $\left(\frac{x+1}{4}\right)^2 + \left(\frac{y-2}{3}\right)^2 = \cos^2 t + \sin^2 t = 1$.
$\left(\frac{x+1}{4}\right)^2 + \left(\frac{y-2}{3}\right)^2 = 1$ is an ellipse centered at $(-1, 2)$ with horizontal major axis 8 and minor axis 6.
e. ellipse centered at (h, k) with axes of lengths $2|a|$ and $2|b|$

4. **a.** ellipse centered at $(0, 0)$ rotated from standard position 45° about the origin
   b. $x = \cos\left(t + \frac{\pi}{4}\right) = \cos t \cdot \cos\frac{\pi}{4} - \sin t \cdot \sin\frac{\pi}{4} = \frac{\sqrt{2}}{2}\cos t - \frac{\sqrt{2}}{2}\sin t$.
   So $\sqrt{2}x + \sin t = \cos t$. But $\sin t = y$, so $\sqrt{2}x + y = \cos t$.
   Hence, $(\sqrt{2}x + y)^2 + y^2 = \cos^2 t + \sin^2 t = 1$. Thus, $2x^2 + \sqrt{2}xy + y^2 + y^2 = 1$, or $x^2 + \sqrt{2}xy + y^2 - \frac{1}{2} = 0$
   c. Predictions will vary.
   d. $\cos\left(t - \frac{\pi}{2}\right) = \sin t$. So $x = \sin t = y$. The figure is the graph of $x = y$ over the range of $\sin t$, −1 to 1.

Calculator Master 1

1. Samples will vary.

Degree	Sample number of turning points
1st	0
2nd	1
3rd	0, 2
4th	1, 3
5th	0, 2, 4

2. a. No
   b. No
   c. A turning point indicates a relative maximum or a relative minimum, so the number of turning points is the same as the number of relative maxima or minima of a function.
3. a. 1, 3, 5
   b. 0, 2, 4, 6
   c. 1, 3, 5, 7
   d. 0, 2, 4, 6, 8
   e. 1, 3, 5, 7, 9
   f. No; a polynomial of even degree can have only an odd number of turning points.
   g. Yes; a polynomial of odd degree has only even numbers of turning points.
   h. maximum: $n - 1$; minimum: 0 if n is odd or 1 if n is even
4. a. Sample: $y = x^6 + x^4 - 6x^2 + 2$
   b. Sample: $y = x^6 - 6x^5 + 6x^4 + 10x^3 - 9x^2 - 7x + 1$

Calculator Master 2

1. a. no
   b. As $x \to \infty$, $f(x) \to \infty$; as $x \to -\infty$, $f(x) \to \infty$.
   c. As $x \to \infty$, $f(x) \to \infty$; as $x \to -\infty$, $f(x) \to -\infty$.
   d. No; in the smaller window, the end behavior of f is not fully apparent because we do not see enough of the graph. Students may question

whether an even larger window is necessary. If they have done Calculator Master 1, they may note that part **b** is not accurate because a 5th degree polynomial cannot have exactly three turning points, and part **c** is accurate because a 5th degree may have at most four turning points.
   e.

x	y
1000	1×10^{14}
1001	1×10^{14}
10000	1×10^{19}
10001	1×10^{19}
100000	1×10^{24}
100001	1×10^{24}
-1000	-1×10^{14}
-999	-1×10^{14}
-10000	-1×10^{19}
-9999	-1×10^{19}
-100000	-1×10^{24}
-99999	-1×10^{24}

Yes; as $x \to \infty$, $f(x) \to \infty$; as $x \to -\infty$, $f(x) \to -\infty$
2. a. As $x \to \infty$, $f(x) \to -\infty$; as $x \to -\infty$, $f(x) \to -\infty$.
   b. As $x \to \infty$, $f(x) \to \infty$; as $x \to -\infty$, $f(x) \to -\infty$.
   c. As $x \to \infty$, $f(x) \to \infty$; as $x \to -\infty$, $f(x) \to \infty$.
   d. The smaller windows do not show enough of the graph to display the true end behavior, although (a) is a plausible answer for a 4th degree polynomial.
   e.

x	y
1000	1×10^{11}
1001	1×10^{11}
10000	1×10^{15}
10001	1×10^{15}
100000	1×10^{19}
100001	1×10^{19}

x	y
-1000	9.9×10^{10}
-999	9.9×10^{10}
-10000	1×10^{15}
-9999	1×10^{15}
-100000	1×10^{19}
-99999	1×10^{19}

Yes; as $x \to \infty$, $f(x) \to \infty$; as $x \to -\infty$, $f(x) \to \infty$
3. Answers will vary. Students should see that graphs provide a good view of the "big picture," but tables can indicate specifics more quickly and efficiently.

Calculator Master 3

1. a. 200 ft/sec; 10°; 8.8 ft/sec
   b. $200(\cos 10°)t - 8.8t$; $-16t^2 + 200(\sin 10°)t$
2. a. about 42 ft away; about 408 ft
   b. 2.2 sec
   c. 18.8 ft
   d. 1.1 sec
   e. 2.17 sec; 408 ft; 1.09 sec; 18.8 ft
   f. about 22 ft
   g. 428 ft; 18.8 ft
3. a. 209.7 ft/sec; 205.2 ft/sec
   b. The one that fights the wind goes higher by about 0.9 ft.
   c. 11.07°; 10.55°
   d. The one that fights the wind goes higher by about 2.1 ft.
4. a. 45°
   b. 1250 ft
   c. 120 ft/sec
   d. 5.3 sec
   e. The ball goes much higher.
   f. 112.5 ft

Calculator Master 4

1. a. $1.2x^4 - 1.34x^3 - 14.17x^2 + 13.36x + 4.2$
   b. $-\dfrac{10}{3}, -\dfrac{1}{4}, \dfrac{6}{5}, \dfrac{7}{2}$

Precalculus and Discrete Mathematics © Scott Foresman Addison Wesley

c. $\left(-\infty, -\frac{10}{3}\right), \left(-\frac{1}{4}, \frac{6}{5}\right),$ $\left(\frac{7}{2}, \infty\right); \left(-\frac{10}{3}, -\frac{1}{4}\right), \left(\frac{6}{5}, \frac{7}{2}\right)$

d. $x < -\frac{10}{3}, -\frac{1}{4} < x < \frac{6}{5},$ $x > \frac{7}{2}$

$-\frac{10}{3} \quad -\frac{1}{4} \quad \frac{6}{5} \quad \frac{7}{2}$

2. a. $0.8x^3 + x^2 - 1.1x + 0.2$

b. $-2, \frac{1}{4}, \frac{1}{2}$

c. $\left[-2, \frac{1}{4}\right], \left[\frac{1}{2}, \infty\right);$ $(-\infty, -2], \left[\frac{1}{4}, \frac{1}{2}\right]$

d. $x \le -2, \frac{1}{4} \le x \le \frac{1}{2}$

$-2 \qquad \frac{1}{4} \;\; \frac{1}{2}$

3. a. $\dfrac{r^2 - 2.7r - 10.08}{r^2 + 2r + 3}$

b. -2.1, 4.8

c. $(-\infty, -2.1], [4.8, \infty);$ [-2.1, 4.8]

d. $r \le -2.1, r \ge 4.8$

$-2.1 \qquad\quad 4.8$

4. a. $5^{x^2} - 3^{(x+2)}$

b. -0.876, 1.559

c. $(-\infty, -0.876),$ $(1.559, \infty);$ $(-0.876, 1.559)$

d. $x < -0.876, x > 1.559$

$-0.876 \quad 1.559$

5. a. $(x + 1)\log_2 x - x^2\log_5 x$

b. 1, 3.077

c. (1, 3.077); (0, 1), (3.077, ∞)

d. $0 < x < 1; x > 3.077$

$0 \quad 1 \qquad 3.077$

Calculator Master 5

1. b. $x \ne 1$
c. 1
2. a. no
b. yes

c. yes

x	y
1000	2003
1001	2005
1002	2007
-1000	-1997
-999	-1995
-998	-1993

3. a. 2
b. $q(x) = 2x + 3$
c. Sample: The line is an asymptote for the graph of f. Or, students may simply notice that the graph of f approaches the line at the extremes.

4. a. $2x^2 + x - 1 =$ $(2x + 3)\cdot(x - 1) + p(1)$
b. Sample: The linear equation is the quotient polynomial when $p(x)$ is divided by $x - c$.
c. 2
d. $2x^2 + x - 1 =$ $2x^2 + x - 3 + 2$
e. $\dfrac{2x^2 + x - 1}{x - 1} =$ $2x + 3 + \dfrac{2}{x - 1}$
f. They appear to coincide.
g. no; $p(c) \ne 0$

5. b. $x \ne -1$
c. -1
6. a. yes
b. yes
c. yes

x	y
1000	1999
1001	2001
1002	2003
-1000	-2001
-999	-1999
-998	-1997

d. $q(x) = 2x - 1$
e. $2x^2 + x - 1 =$ $(2x - 1)(x + 1) + p(-1)$

f. $p(-1) = 0;$ $2x^2 + x - 1 =$ $2x^2 + x - 1 + 0$
g. $\dfrac{2x^2 + x - 1}{x + 1} =$ $2x - 1 + \dfrac{0}{x + 1}$
h. They appear to coincide.
i. yes; $p(c) = 0$
j. If the graph shows a vertical and/or an oblique asymptote, then $x - c$ is not a factor. If the graph looks identical to a line, then $x - c$ is a factor. (But there will be a hole in the latter's graph.)

7. a. $q(x) = -2x - 1;$ $p(c) = -4;$ no
b. $q(x) = 3x + 2;$ $p(c) = -4;$ no
c. $q(x) = -3x + 1;$ $p(c) = 0;$ yes

Calculator Master 6

1. a. 2, -6, and 5
b. $2x^2 - 6x + 5$
c. -3
2. a. $q(x) = 4x^4 - x^3 +$ $x^2 - 3x + 2; r(x) = -1$
b. $q(x) = 4x^3 + 2x^2 - 2;$ $r(x) = 0$
c. yes, in part **b**. The remainder is 0.
3. a. The coefficient of x in the divisor $\ne 1$.
b. The coefficient of x in the new divisor $= 1$.
c. $x^3 - 6x + 1$
d. 7
4. c. $q(x) = x^4 - 12x^3 + 2;$ $r(x) = -16$

Calculator Master 7

1. a. composite
b. prime
c. prime
d. composite
e. part **c**; It required many more divisions.
f. If $D \le \sqrt{N}$
g. Yes; sample: The program may divide by a multiple of a divisor

already tried. If a number is not a divisor, any multiple of it also is not a divisor.

2. a. Sample: 329
   b. Sample: 448
   c. 28 and 496
   d. If the factor sum is 1, the number is prime.
   e. If $n = 5$, $2^n - 1 = 31$, which is prime. Then $2^{n-1}(2^n - 1) = 2^4(2^5 - 1) = 16 \cdot 31 = 496$. The factor sum of 496 is 496.
   f. Each number is the factor sum of the other.

3. a. $5096 = 2^3 \cdot 7^2 \cdot 13$; 4423 is prime; $271{,}793 = 191 \cdot 1423$
   b. Divide 6644321 by 857. The answer should be an integer.
   c. 857 and 7753; It took much longer than the task in part **b**.
   d. Prediction will vary.

Calculator Master 8

1. a. As $x \to \infty$, $r(x) \to 0$; as $x \to -\infty$, $t(x) \to 0$.
   b. yes; $y = 0$

2. a.
   TABLE 1

	x	y
f	1000	0.00201
	-1000	-0.00199
g	1000	0.00199
	-1000	-0.00201
h	1000	0.00100
	-1000	-0.00100
k	1000	0.00099
	-1000	-0.00101

   b. yes

c.
TABLE 2

	V.A.	O.A.	H.A.	Zeros
f	$x = 5$; $x = -2$	none	$y = 0$	$-\frac{1}{2}$
g	$x = -3$	none	$y = 0$	$-\frac{1}{2}$
h	$x = -2$	none	$y = 0$	no real
k	none	none	$y = 0$	5

d–f. See Tables 1 and 2.

3. a. $f(x) = \dfrac{2x + 1}{(x + 2)(x - 5)}$
   There are vertical asymptotes at $x = -2$ and $x = 5$ because these values make the denominator zero, and they do not make the numerator zero.
   b. numerator. There is a zero at $x = -\frac{1}{2}$ because this value makes the numerator zero.
   c. $g(x) = \dfrac{2x + 1}{(x + 3)(x + 3)}$
   There is only one vertical asymptote at $x = -3$ because only this value makes the denominator zero; there is a zero at $x = -\frac{1}{2}$ because this value makes the numerator zero.
   $h(x) = \dfrac{x - 5}{(x + 2)(x - 5)}$
   There is a vertical asymptote only at $x = -2$ because the identical factors of $x - 5$ in numerator and denominator produce a removable discontinuity at $x = 5$; there are no values that make the numerator zero independent of the denominator, so there are no zeros.
   $k(x) = \dfrac{x - 5}{x^2 + 2x + 3}$

There are no vertical asymptotes because no values make the denominator zero; there is a zero at $x = 5$ because this value makes the numerator zero.

4. a. As $x \to \infty$, $r(x) \to \infty$; as $x \to -\infty$, $r(x) \to -\infty$. Or, as $x \to \infty$, $r(x) \to -\infty$; as $x \to -\infty$, $r(x) \to \infty$.
   b. no. The end behavior of the function does not approach a limiting value as x approaches ∞ or $-\infty$.
   c.
   TABLE 3

	x	y
q	1000	1001
	-1000	-999
r	1000	-996
	-1000	1004

   TABLE 4

	V.A.	O.A.	H.A.	Zeros
q	$x = 4$	$y = x + 1$	none	-2; 5
r	$x = 2$	$y = -x + 1$	none	3

   d. no. Both types of asymptotes are determined by the end behavior of the function: if the function approaches a limiting value as x approaches $\pm\infty$, then the asymptotes will be horizontal. If the function does not approach a limiting value as x approaches $\pm\infty$, then the function does not approach a limiting value and may have an oblique asymptote.
   e. yes. The oblique asymptote is determined by the end behavior. The vertical occurs when the denominator $= 0$ and the numerator $\neq 0$.

Precalculus and Discrete Mathematics © Scott Foresman Addison Wesley

Calculator Master 9

1. a. $24 + 38 + \dfrac{40}{x}$

   b. 145 min

   c. $24 + 38 + \dfrac{40}{x} = 145$

2. a. yes. The intersection of Y_1 and Y_2 is visible.

   b. .482; Lena's biking speed must be at least .482 km/min for her to meet her goal.

   c. about 3.7%

3. a. no

   b. It will decrease to $\dfrac{24}{1.03}$ or about 23.3 min.

   c. It will decrease to $\dfrac{38}{1.03}$ or about 36.9 min.

   d. .472 km/min; yes

4. a. $\dfrac{23.4}{1 + p} + \dfrac{84.2}{1 + 2p} + \dfrac{37.3}{1 + 2p}$

   b. $\dfrac{23.4}{1 + p} + \dfrac{84.2}{1 + 2p} + \dfrac{37.3}{1 + 2p} = 141.75$

c. 3; the one in the first quadrant

d. .012; Lena should increase this year's swimming speed by at least 1.2% and each of the other speeds by 2.4% in order to tie or beat this year's winning time.

Calculator Master 10

1. All possible identities:

$\cos\left(x + \dfrac{\pi}{2}\right) = \sin(x + \pi)$

$\cos\left(x + \dfrac{\pi}{2}\right) = \sin(x - \pi)$

$\cos\left(x - \dfrac{\pi}{2}\right) = \sin(\pi - x)$

$\cos\left(x - \dfrac{\pi}{2}\right) = \sin(x + 2\pi)$

$\cos\left(x - \dfrac{\pi}{2}\right) = \sin(x - 2\pi)$

$\cos(x + \pi) = \sin\left(x - \dfrac{\pi}{2}\right)$

$\cos(x + \pi) = \sin\left(\dfrac{3\pi}{2} - x\right)$

$\cos(x - \pi) = \sin\left(x - \dfrac{\pi}{2}\right)$

$\cos(x - \pi) = \sin\left(\dfrac{3\pi}{2} - x\right)$

$\cos(x + 2\pi) = \sin\left(x + \dfrac{\pi}{2}\right)$

$\cos(x + 2\pi) = \sin\left(\dfrac{\pi}{2} - x\right)$

$\cos\left(\dfrac{\pi}{2} - x\right) = \sin(\pi - x)$

$\cos\left(\dfrac{\pi}{2} - x\right) = \sin(x + 2\pi)$

$\cos\left(\dfrac{\pi}{2} - x\right) = \sin(x - 2\pi)$

$\cos(\pi - x) = \sin\left(x - \dfrac{\pi}{2}\right)$

$\cos(\pi - x) = \sin\left(\dfrac{3\pi}{2} - x\right)$

$\cos\left(\dfrac{3\pi}{2} - x\right) = \sin(x + \pi)$

$\cos\left(\dfrac{3\pi}{2} - x\right) = \sin(x - \pi)$

$\cos(2\pi - x) = \sin\left(x + \dfrac{\pi}{2}\right)$

$\cos(2\pi - x) = \sin\left(\dfrac{\pi}{2} - x\right)$

2. Proofs will vary.

Calculator Master 11

1. a. The terms of the sequence reached values beyond the range of the calculator.

   b. ∞

   c. 0

   d.

a_1	2	$\frac{1}{2}$	1	.99	1.01	-1	-1.01	0	-.7
$\lim\limits_{n \to \infty} a_n$	∞	0	1	0	∞	1	∞	0	0

   e. For $|a_1| > 1$, $\lim\limits_{n \to \infty} a_n = \infty$; for $|a_1| = 1$, $\lim\limits_{n \to \infty} a_n = 1$; for $|a_1| < 1$, $\lim\limits_{n \to \infty} a_n = 0$.

   f. 0, 1

2. a. -2, 3

3. a. $\dfrac{1 \pm \sqrt{3}}{2}$; 1.366025404 or -.366025404

   b. The calculator did not compute with the exact values of the fixed points, so eventually, the terms of the sequence reached values beyond the range of the calculator.

   c.

a_1	2	$\frac{1 + \sqrt{3}}{2}$	1	.5	$\frac{1 - \sqrt{3}}{2}$	-1	-2
$\lim\limits_{n \to \infty} a_n$	∞	1.366	-.366	-.366	-.366	-.366	∞

d. Sample:

a_1	1.3661	1.3660	-.3660	-.3661	-1.3660	-1.3661
$\lim\limits_{n\to\infty} a_n$	∞	-.3660	-.3660	-.3660	-.3660	∞

For $|a_1| < \dfrac{1+\sqrt{3}}{2}$, $\lim\limits_{n\to\infty} a_n = -.3660$; for $|a_1| > \dfrac{1+\sqrt{3}}{2}$, $\lim\limits_{n\to\infty} a_n = \infty$.

4. a. $\dfrac{1 \pm \sqrt{5}}{2}$ (1.618033989 or -.618033989)

b. Sample:

a_1	2	$\frac{1+\sqrt{5}}{2}$	1	.5	0	-.5	$\frac{1-\sqrt{5}}{2}$	-1	-2
behavior	$\lim\limits_{n\to\infty} a_n = \infty$	$a_n = \frac{1+\sqrt{5}}{2}$	alt. between 0 and -1	alt. between 0 and -1	alt. between 0 and -1	alt. between 0 and -1	$a_n = \frac{1-\sqrt{5}}{2}$	alt. between 0 and 1	$\lim\limits_{n\to\infty} a_n = \infty$

c. The sequence 0, -1, 0, -1, . . . , repeats after every 2 iterations of n.

5. a. Sample:

a_1	2	$\frac{5+\sqrt{155}}{10}$	1.7449	1	0	-.7449	$\frac{5-\sqrt{155}}{10}$	-1	-2
behavior	$\lim\limits_{n\to\infty} a_n = \infty$	$a_n = \frac{5+\sqrt{155}}{10}$	*	*	*	*	$a_n = \frac{5-\sqrt{155}}{10}$	*	$\lim\limits_{n\to\infty} a_n = \infty$

*Alternates between .0194, −1.2996, .3890, −1.1487

b. .0194, -1.2996, .3890, -1.1487

c. 4

6. a. Sample:

a_1	3	2.1	2	1.9	1.1	1	.9
behavior	$\lim\limits_{n\to\infty} a_n = \infty$	$\lim\limits_{n\to\infty} a_n = \infty$	2	*	*	-1	*

a_1	0	-.5	-1	-1.5	-2	-3
behavior	2	*	-1	*	2	$\lim\limits_{n\to\infty} a_n = \infty$

*No apparent pattern

b. No

Calculator Master 12

1. a. a is the length of each petal. The number of petals is n if n is odd and $2n$ if n is even.

b. Sample: The x-axis bisects one of the petals of $r = \cos 3\theta$; the y-axis bisects one of the petals of $r = \sin 3\theta$.

c. Sample: The axes bisect 4 petals of $r = \cos 4\theta$; the axes do not bisect any petals of $r = \sin 4\theta$.

d. Sample: If n is odd, the x-axis bisects one of the petals of $r = \cos n\theta$, and the y-axis bisects one of the petals of $r = \sin n\theta$. If n is even, the axes bisect all the petals of $r = \cos n\theta$, and the axes do not bisect any petals of $r = \sin n\theta$.

2. a. The second graph is the image of the first under a rotation of $\dfrac{\pi}{4}$ around the pole.

b. The second graph is the image of the first under a rotation of $\dfrac{\pi}{8}$ around the pole.

c. The second graph is the image of the first under a rotation of $\dfrac{\pi}{k}$ around the pole.

3. a. Two petals of length 1 bisected by the x-axis

b. a is the length of the petal.

c. Sample:
$$r^2 = \sin 2\left(\theta + \frac{\pi}{4}\right)$$

d. Sample:
$$r^2 = \cos 2\left(\theta - \frac{\pi}{4}\right)$$

Calculator Master 13

1. **a.** (3, -3); (5, 5)
   b. 4
   c. $b = -15$; $y = 4x - 15$

2.

Δx	slope	y-int.	eqn.
2	4	-15	$y = 4x - 15$
1	3	-12	$y = 3x - 12$
.5	2.5	-10.5	$y = 2.5x - 10.5$
.1	2.1	-9.3	$y = 2.1x - 9.3$
.01	2.01	-9.03	$y = 2.01x - 9.03$
-.01	1.99	-8.97	$y = 1.99x - 8.97$
-.1	1.9	-8.7	$y = 1.9x - 8.7$
-.5	1.5	-7.5	$y = 1.5x - 7.5$
-1	1	-6	$y = x - 6$
-2	0	0	$y = -3$

3. **a.** Sample: $y = 2.5x - 10.5$ and $y = 2.1x - 9.3$.
   b. no; Sample: $y = 2.1x - 9.3$ still looks tangent.
   c. $y = 1.9x - 8.7$

4. **a.** 2
   b. $\lim\limits_{x \to \infty} \dfrac{(3 + \Delta x)^2 - 4(3 + \Delta x) - (3^2 - 4 \cdot 3)}{\Delta x} = \dfrac{9 + 6\Delta x + (\Delta x)^2 - 12 - 4\Delta x + 3}{\Delta x}$

   $= \dfrac{2\Delta x + (\Delta x)^2}{\Delta x} = 2 + \Delta x = 2$

   c. 2
   d. $y = 2x - 9$
   f. 2

5. **a.** -2
   b. $\lim\limits_{x \to \infty} \dfrac{\frac{1}{2}(2 + \Delta x)^2 - 4(2 + \Delta x) - (\frac{1}{2} \cdot 2^2 - 4 \cdot 2)}{\Delta x} = \dfrac{\frac{1}{2}(4 + 4\Delta x + (\Delta x)^2) - 8 - 4\Delta x + 6}{\Delta x}$

   $= \dfrac{-2\Delta x + \frac{1}{2}(\Delta x)^2}{\Delta x} = -2 + \frac{1}{2}\Delta x = -2$

   c. 0; $y = -8$
   d. $y = 2x - 18$
   e. $y = 6x - 50$

Calculator Master 14

* Indicates results of simulation, which will vary.

1. **a.** 36
   b. 22*

2. **a.**

l	c	p	t*
2	10	100	124
2	20	400	388
2	30	900	1016

   b. $p \approx t$
   c. $p = c^2$
   d. p is multiplied by 4.
   e. p is multiplied by 9.

3. **a.**

l	c	p	t*
3	6	216	280
3	10	1000	1141
3	20	8000	6033
3	30	27,000	19,138

Precalculus and Discrete Mathematics © Scott Foresman Addison Wesley

b. $p = c^3$; when c is doubled, p is multiplied by 8; when c is tripled, p is multiplied by 27.

4. a.

l	p, when $c = 6$	p, when $c = 10$
2	36	100
3	216	1000
4	1296	10,000
5	5184	100,000
6	31,104	1,000,000

p, when $c = 20$	p, when $c = 30$
400	900
8000	27,000
160,000	810,000
3,200,000	24,300,000
64,000,000	729,000,000

p, when $c = 40$
1600
64,000
2,560,000
102,400,000
4,096,000,000

b. $p = c^l$
c. squaring
d. cubing
e. A 6-number lottery with 10 choices each has $10^6 = 1,000,000$ possibilities; a 3-number lottery with 100 choices each has $100^3 = 1,000,000$ possibilities.

5. a. Lottery A; Lottery A has 64,000 possibilities; Lottery B has 160,000 possibilities.
b. Lottery B; Lottery A has 46,656 possibilities; Lottery B has 10,000 possibilities.

Calculator Master 15

1. a. Sample: 11
b. 10
c. Sample:

T	H	R
10	5	0.5
20	11	0.55
50	28	0.56
100	46	0.46
200	102	0.51

d. 0.5
2. a. Predictions will vary.
b. Sample:

10 Experiments		
K	N	R
0		0
1	I	0.1
2	II	0.2
3	II	0.2
4	IIII	0.4
5	I	0.1
6		0

c. Samples:

20 Experiments		
K	N	R
0	I	0.05
1	I	0.05
2	IIII	0.2
3	JHT I	0.3
4	JHT	0.25
5	III	0.15
6		0

50 Experiments		
K	N	R
0	II	0.04
1	JHT	0.10
2	JHT JHT II	0.24
3	JHT JHT IIII	0.28
4	JHT JHT JHT I	0.32
5		0
6	I	0.02

3. a.

K	$P(K)$
0	0.02
1	0.10
2	0.23
3	0.31
4	0.23
5	0.10
6	0.02

b. Answers will vary. As the number of experiments increases, R will likely get closer to P.
c. The relative frequencies out of a greater number of experiments should match the calculated probabilities more closely.

Precalculus and Discrete Mathematics © Scott Foresman Addison Wesley

Calculator Master 16

1. a.

$$\begin{bmatrix} .99744 & .00048 & .00139 & .00069 \\ .00045 & .99705 & .00171 & .00079 \\ .00096 & .00183 & .99569 & .00512 \\ .00027 & .00089 & .00178 & .99706 \end{bmatrix}$$

b. [.196 ,235 .350 .219]

c. 19.60%; 23.52%; 34.96%; 21.92%

d.

	2000	2010	2020
Northeast	19.60%	19.60%	19.59%
Midwest	23.62%	23.84%	24.05%
South	34.78%	34.36%	33.97%
West	22.00%	22.20%	22.39%

2. a.

$$\begin{bmatrix} .98728 & .00241 & .00688 & .00344 \\ .00224 & .98538 & .00845 & .00393 \\ .00475 & .00904 & .97871 & .00751 \\ .00136 & .00443 & .00879 & .98542 \end{bmatrix}$$

b. yes

c. Sample: $k = 5000$;

$$\begin{bmatrix} .18089 & .28038 & .27748 & .26125 \\ .18089 & .28038 & .27748 & .26125 \\ .18089 & .28038 & .27748 & .26125 \\ .18089 & .28038 & .27748 & .26125 \end{bmatrix}$$

d. Sample: After 5000 years, the population distribution will be: Northeast, 18.09%; Midwest, 28.04%; South, 27.75%; West, 26.13%

e. Sample: Northeast, 18.09%; Midwest, 28.04%; South, 27.75%; West, 26.13%

f. Sample: Northeast, 18.09%; Midwest, 28.04%; South, 27.75%; West, 26.13%

g. no; no; Sample explanation: Many factors could affect population over 5000 years. In fact, the country itself could be different or nonexistent.

3. a. $P = [.42 \ .58]$; $T = \begin{bmatrix} .977 & .023 \\ .011 & .989 \end{bmatrix}$

b. Find k for which T^k is a stochastic matrix with nearly identical rows; only T is needed.

c. 32.35%; 67.65%

Calculator Master 17

1. a. (3, 1)

b. A segment is produced, not a line.

c.

Point	t	x	y
Q_0	0	-2	3
Q_1	1	1	4
Q_2	2	4	5
Q_3	3	7	6

c., e., f.

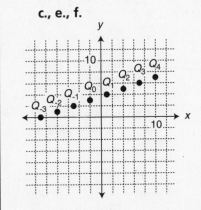

d. Add 3 units to the previous x-coordinate and 1 unit to the previous y-coordinate; that is, add the components of $\vec{v}$ to Q_t to get Q_{t+1}.

e. (10, 7)

f.

Point	t	x	y
Q_{-1}	-1	-5	2
Q_{-2}	-2	-8	1
Q_{-3}	-3	-11	0

g. Change Tmin and Tmax. Sample: Tmin = -3, Tmax = 4

h. No, because points are only shown for $t = -3$ to $t = 4$.

2. a. More points are plotted so the line looks more "filled in."

b. Sample: 0.07

c. no; there are still separate points but they are very close together.

d. $\dfrac{1}{3}$

e. slope = $\dfrac{y\text{-component}}{x\text{-component}} = \dfrac{v_1}{v_2} = \dfrac{1}{3}$

f. $\dfrac{x+2}{3} = t$; $y = \dfrac{1}{3}x + \dfrac{11}{3}$

g. $\dfrac{1}{3}$

3. a. (4, -2); (-3, 2)

c. Add -3 to the x-coordinate and add 2 to the y-coordinate; add the components of $\vec{v}$.

d. $y = -\dfrac{2}{3}x + \dfrac{2}{3}$; slope = $\dfrac{y\text{-component}}{x\text{-component}} = \dfrac{v_1}{v_2} = \dfrac{2}{-3}$

4. a. $x = x_o + v_1 t$; $y = y_o + v_2 t$

b. Add v_1 to the x-coordinate and add v_2 to the y-coordinate.

c. $y = \dfrac{v_2}{v_1}x = \left(y - \dfrac{v_2 x_o}{v_1}\right)$;

slope = $\dfrac{v_1}{v_2}$

Calculator Master 18

1. a. URS: 17.375; LRS: 12.875

b–c.

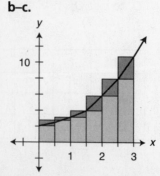

d. $h = 9$; $w = \dfrac{1}{2}$; $A = \dfrac{9}{2}$

2. a.

n	LRS	URS	E
6	12.875	17.375	4.5
10	13.695	16.395	2.7
50	14.732	15.272	.54
100	14.865	15.135	.27
1000	14.987	15.014	.027

b. $E \cdot n = 27$; $E = \dfrac{27}{n}$

c. $9 \cdot \dfrac{3}{n} = \dfrac{27}{n}$

d. URS − LRS = $15.135 - 14.865 =$ $.27 = \dfrac{27}{100}$

3. a.

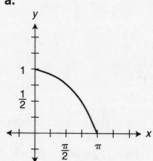

b.

n	LRS	URS	E
10	1.839	2.153	.314
50	1.968	2.031	.063
100	1.984	2.016	.032
1000	1.998	2.002	.004

c. $E = \dfrac{\pi}{n}$

d. 1

e. $w = \dfrac{\pi}{n}$; $A = 1 \cdot \dfrac{\pi}{n} = \dfrac{\pi}{n}$

f. URS − LRS = $2.016 - 1.984 = .032 \approx$ $\dfrac{\pi}{100}$

g. $\dfrac{\pi}{n} \le .0001$; $n \ge \dfrac{\pi}{.0001}$; $n \ge 31{,}416$

URS − LRS = $2.00005 - 1.99995 = .000100$

Calculator Master 19

1. a. π

b. Predictions will vary.

2. a. $0 \le \theta \le \dfrac{\pi}{2}$

b. $\dfrac{\pi}{2n}$

c. $\dfrac{\pi}{2n}$, $2 \cdot \dfrac{\pi}{2n} = \dfrac{\pi}{n}$; $\dfrac{3\pi}{2n}$; $\dfrac{i\pi}{2n}$

d. $\dfrac{1}{2}(\sin 2\theta_i)^2 \cdot \dfrac{\pi}{2n}$

e. $\displaystyle\sum_{i=1}^{n} \dfrac{1}{2}(\sin 2\theta_i)^2 \cdot \dfrac{\pi}{2n}$

3. a. no

b. .3926990817

c. 1.571

d. $\dfrac{\pi}{2}$; comments will vary.

4. a. 8

b. $0 \le \theta \le \dfrac{\pi}{4}$

c. 1.571 or $\dfrac{\pi}{2}$

d. 8

e. $0 \le \theta \le \dfrac{\pi}{6}$; 1.571 or $\dfrac{\pi}{2}$

Precalculus and Discrete Mathematics © Scott Foresman Addison Wesley